CHILDLESS
LIVING

*The Joys and Challenges
of Life without Children*

LISETTE SCHUITEMAKER

FINDHORN PRESS

Findhorn Press
One Park Street
Rochester, Vermont 05767
www.findhornpress.com

Findhorn Press is a division of Inner Traditions International

Cataloging-in-Publication Data for this title is available from the Library of Congress

ISBN 978-1-62055-838-6 (print)
ISBN 978-1-62055-839-3 (ebook)

Printed and bound in the United States by Versa Press, Inc.

10 9 8 7 6 5 4 3 2 1

Edited by Aimée Warmerdam (concept) and Nicky Leach (text)
Text design and layout by Geoff Green Book Design
This book was typeset in Romulus

To send correspondence to the author of this book, mail a first-class letter to the author
c/o Inner Traditions • Bear & Company, One Park Street, Rochester, VT 05767, USA,
and we will forward the communication, or contact the author directly at
www.lisetteschuitemaker.com.

Contents

Spring
Promise and Potential

Summer
Growth and Action

Introduction

We, people without children, are in the news these days. Articles are published regularly on millennials who profess their certainty of not going on to copy the life of their parents. Journalists comment on the remarkable number of political leaders in Europe who have no children of their own. Essays are written on how far people are willing to go in order to fulfil their wish to have children and where we as a society would, could, or should draw the line. Scientists, politicians, and the media alike make comments on how many we, the childless and the childfree, actually are.

Like a ship that appears out of the mist we emerge, and suddenly, we prove to be a flotilla of vessels of all kinds. Our fleet consists of motorboats of marvellous young people who want a family—sure, one day, but not right now; someday in an unspecified later, when we are ready. For the time being, as young adults, we wish to enjoy our flexibility, to discover ourselves and our potential. We want to continue to be able to close the door and be off for a weekend, a few weeks, or a year. We can hardly imagine what will make us give up this delicious freedom one day. Hormones, we imagine. The pressure of family or friends, perhaps. Or the heart becoming curious about the child that could come into existence out of our love.

In our midst, we have sturdy tugboats of those of us who have consciously decided to spread our love wider than predominantly amongst offspring of our own. These mariners generally work full time, and are happy to fill in for colleagues apologetically rushing out, because the childcare centre is about to close or exhausted grandparents need to be relieved from duty. When it is generally assumed that we will be the ones to remain and finish the task at hand, a sense of resentment may start to build within us. Arguing that our free time is as valuable as that of colleagues who chose to have children will not go down well, we know; nor will any suggestion that we too should be eligible for a sabbatical or the childless person's equivalent of maternity and paternity leave.

The solitary ones amongst us come in silent canoes. We love to keep our own company. We revel in the peace and quiet in our homes and in our heads. We wish to apply ourselves to our own interests. Some of us have enough self-awareness to know that we are not parent material, never were. Others may still flirt with the idea, if only we would meet the right partner.

Pairs paddle in nimble double kayaks, in which we may be silent for long stretches of time, each to our own, one not impinging on the space of the other, yet deeply engaged in each other's existence. We are the couples who stimulate each other to lead the life we were meant to lead, whether we had wanted to have children together or not. We make sure we have a good time, just the two of us.

Slender vessels emerge, navigated by those amongst us who would have loved to have children, but to whom these were not given. A few of us immediately changed tack when our seed proved too weak, our ovulation problematic, or other impediments stood in the way of conception. Others took a long time to come to terms with this fate, as friends left and right seemed to conceive without any problem at all, so why didn't we? Over time, we charted a new course for a life full of meaningful work, volunteering, and other people's children with whom we could share our life experiences.

In some instances, we have not given up, but continued to try for years on end to make the impossible happen. Using today's latest technologies, we had hoped time and again that our efforts to achieve pregnancy and carry it to term would pay off. In our despair, going for one more last attempt, some of us have crossed lines we never thought we would cross. Still others find, somewhat to our surprise, that we were actually relieved when gestation didn't happen. Maybe in our heart of hearts we knew, but hadn't quite dared to concede even to ourselves, that parenting didn't really attract us. We thought it was mandatory. We were afraid to be considered weird, so we tried to suppress our impetus towards a more unconventional lifestyle, which we are now free to pursue.

Silent schooners abound, bearing those born in times when, or places where, there is or was shame in being childless, so talking about this topic was simply not done. Hardly ever did those of us in the same boat speak with each other, family members, or close friends about this vital theme in our lives. We kept mum. We pretended all was well. We ranted and raved in private. We felt alone with our perplexing predicament, and slowly, we accepted the way our cookie crumbled. But a sense of mourning for the life we didn't get never leaves us completely and, especially in crunch times, this rears its head and leaves us feeling alone all over again.

Hydrofoils carry those of us who walk a spiritual path. In our dedication to the One, having a family, and in some cases even a relationship, would be a distraction. Although not easy at times, we find joy in our faith and in the work we do, seeing it as an expression of our one big love for the divine.

Lifeboats are navigated by a rapidly growing number of us who worry about the role of humanity in the degradation of the earth. We see overpopulation as the main cause of the multiple crises of climate change, food scarcity, drinking water shortages, extinction of species, and decreasing biodiversity. We don't wish to add our bit to those global problems by bringing yet another consumer onto a planet that is already heavily burdened.

Champions of emancipation and feminism are at the helm of pilot vessels that guide women worldwide to a different existence from the traditional one of mother and wife. This group of us has bravely fought for equal rights and opportunities under the law, demonstrated tirelessly against abuse and exploitation of women and minority groups, and advocated for sexual self-determination to be accepted as the norm by the next generation, and the fight isn't over yet.

Invisible in this flotilla are the submarines in which some of us travel into deep waters, below the radar, our legacies noticed only by the few with whom we keep close. We do our work, we have our interests, we make our contribution, and secretly, we are terrified that no one will be there for us in the end. Yet, there was and is no other way for us. This is our life.

Cruise ships form part of our fleet, too, filled with aunts and uncles vacationing outside of school holidays. Our lifestyles offer nieces, nephews, and other young friends examples of lives that differ from those of their own families. We listen to their stories about struggles with parents, the dynamics within the family. We are able to see them for who they are because we don't need to raise them; they see us for who we are because they don't need to project their hopes, fears, and frustrations onto us as they do on their parents.

Sturdy barges are manned by those of us with a beloved who had children already and who, after divorce or death of their former partner, didn't want to start over again. We haven't always been welcomed with open arms in those broken homes. We have had to learn the fine art of tacking during those times when we couldn't travel straight as the crow flies. We've had to sit on our hands, as we were not the parents but the live-in-partner, the stepmum, or surrogate father, and no matter how much we cared, we didn't have the authority of the biological parent. Many of us, however, find our way and come into a loving relationship with our partner's children. When they in turn become parents, the grandchildren do not distinguish between who is of their blood and who has come later; they love us all the same.

Feluccas are sailed by the women amongst us who never married, and thus avoided the whole discussion about whether or not to have children. The question we get asked the most is why we were so adamant to go solo. We have other things to do, we respond. Our yearning is to work, to be independent, to be our own bosses.

On private yachts, we find the hedonists who work hard, earn well, and love to party. Enjoying weekends away has been our privilege ever since we decided never to be knee deep in nappies or required to ferry the children to and fro.

In the second half of our lives, old friends appear on the quay. Their children are grown up and have left the parental home, so they have more time on their hands now. We drop down the gangway and welcome them aboard our free and full existence. We are interested in stories about their children and pictures of their grandchildren, sure; but in moderation. You can't blame us for that, and those who do will soon lose their standing invitation to come aboard.

So it is that those of us without children navigate our own yachts, barges, skiffs, sloops, windjammers, or dories, each with our own course and our own story. What we have in common is that we have more explaining to do to ourselves and to others than people who follow the path of parenthood.

Deviating from the norm, we also share a number of qualities. We like to weave our lives in non-traditional patterns. We are autonomous and unconventional. With no little one needing to be fed, clothed, taken to school, kept with the program, and provided for, we are self-starters. We are self-directed, as we have to find reasons within ourselves to rise and leave the house to smell the freshness of the air and go to the market to get the groceries in. We must be able to enjoy our own company when, for long stretches of time, no others are around to talk to, share a meal, or watch a movie with. We are self-sufficient, and as we are the only ones to make sure we live a meaningful life, we are or need to cultivate the quality of being self-fulfilling.

Why This Book

The idea for this book sprang from an unexpected and beautifully candid conversation at the launch of one of my previous books, *The Eldest Daughter Effect,* in London in November 2016. I began my session talking about the stories we tell ourselves as eldest daughters, saying that I had not found it easy to be the firstborn and that this was one of the reasons for not having had children of my own. Other women chimed in that they had no children either, and we were off to a level of intimacy that had all of us sharing deeply, those with and without children alike.

This exquisite exchange kept swirling through me, and when I started to look around, I was surprised by how many people without children I actually knew. Three out of six cousins on my father's side of the family have not procreated. Neither my partner nor one of his sisters ever wanted children. His three other siblings had six children altogether, two of whom have no offspring. Five of my ten dearest women friends have no children. Some of them had imagined a family of their own when they were young. I knew that much, but I also realized I didn't really know the details of their past or any trepidation they might have about the future.

Once I settled on this topic, I started to have conversations with friends we had never had before. Nor was it difficult, it turned out, to find people willing to talk about the why, how, and what of their childlessness or their choice not to go for parenthood. I admit to even feeling flooded at some point by snowballing friends of friends who had never spoken about their childless life much—people who found me through my posts on social media, complete strangers at parties who confessed their life journeys to me.

I was initiated into the innermost sanctuaries of people's secret thoughts about themselves and their choices. I was invited into abysses of loneliness and doubt below lives that looked good on the surface. I was inspired by the dedication of people who had always known that having children was not on their life path. Overall, I was touched by the amount of love the majority of us, people without children, bring to our work, our volunteering, our community, our family and friends, young people in our lives, our pets, our gardens, our chance encounters with strangers, books we write, places we visit, art we admire, music we enjoy, boards we sit on, our own home, and being alone doing whatever.

Bizarrely Happy

In an ideal world, I would have had a conversation with at least one person from every corner of the planet, so I decided to design a survey to do this for me. At a dinner for professional women, I met data researcher Marian Dragt. In a relationship with a woman, and happily without children herself, she immediately said yes when I asked if she would be willing to professionalize my research.

I approached her with a questionnaire I had put together intuitively, based on my own experience, conversations I was starting to have, and books on the topic that I had begun to read. In three efficient sessions, we compiled a survey that we tested on friends in four different countries, adapted, and posted on social media and my website. Six weeks later, when we met to go over the results, Marian Dragt was smiling widely.

"You have reached a bizarrely happy segment of the world population," she said, as she made us a big pot of tea. "They are extraordinarily pleased with their lives, their own development, and the contribution they feel they make to society."

Having had 715 people start on the survey, with 502 completing most of the personal details, we had gathered what professionals call "a convenient sample". Marian Dragt looked at me sternly—this petite woman whose brain is wired to mine data at lightning speed, who is passionate about using technology to give people better insights and who, above all, loves to sing baroque music with her clear mezzo-soprano voice. I saw her eyes twinkle behind her glasses as she tried to impress upon me that I couldn't generalize from the data we had assembled, since we had only done the survey once and without a control group.

She showed me the list of our respondents' countries. My compatriots from the Netherlands were in the lead, with 171 participants, followed by 78 from the United States, 61 from the United Kingdom, 57 from Italy, 16 from Australia, and 14 from Canada. Single digit numbers of respondents came from Belgium, Switzerland, Germany, Colombia, Ireland, Japan, France, Mexico, Brazil, Sweden, India, Denmark, Poland, and Egypt. We had one person each from China, Costa Rica, Mauritius, Nepal, New Zealand, Nigeria, the Philippines, Spain, Thailand, and the Ukraine. All in all, to my delight, people from 30 countries had participated.

Not all of them had filled out the question about gender, but of the ones who did, 53 were men, 444 women, and 5 different. They indicated that they didn't really experience pressure from within their family, culture, or religion about not having children. They divided themselves evenly between being introvert and extrovert. When it came to negative feelings, such as envy of those with children or grandchildren, regrets about the course of their lives, or anxiety about their old age, most people responded by marking either Disagree or Neutral. This was in line with the questions on positive feelings about realizing their potential and how valued they feel.

"With such a bizarrely happy sample," Marian Dragt remarked, whilst sorting the data in a format I could handle, "I would gather that the sense of fulfilment these people feel corresponds with your own."

I hadn't seen that one coming, but she was right on the mark. Although I am aware that I cannot fathom the depth of the love between a parent and a child, I am grateful every day that I do not have children. I feel deep appreciation for having had the stubbornness and courage to follow my own path, and I couldn't feel more grateful for the experiences I have allowed myself to gather. Of course, if I had become a mother, I would have gained other experiences, and had parenthood been part of my life path, that would have been perfect. As it is, I feel complete and happy and not missing out on anything. Quite the contrary: I feel as rich as can be in my childless and now also grandchildless existence.

An Unspoken Topic

The choice not to have children, whether made intentionally or against our will, travels with us throughout our lives. This is how I came to describe childless living through the lens of the four annual seasons.

Not all of us will make it to the age of a 100, but each season of our life spans about 25 years. Spring stands for the early years, when so much is still possible, when we are finding out who we are and what kind of life will suit us best. In summer, remaining childless through circumstance or childfree by choice will put us on a different course from that of most people. Becoming who we are, we will find new friends, new outlets for our love and dedication, and perhaps joyfully take on the role of aunt or uncle. Autumn signifies the time of harvesting. Experienced and wise, we may be at the height of our powers in our work, our discernment, and in what we can convey to younger people we befriend in our personal and professional lives. Then winter comes, when many parents, it is true, rely on their children to look after them, and we will have to be engaging enough for others to want to visit and help us, when we can no longer help ourselves.

You will meet many people in this book. I conducted over 70 interviews with people from their twenties up to their nineties from 16 countries. I also had innumerable casual conversations wherever I went these past two years. When I mentioned what I was researching, people took me aside and told me their own stories or those of close friends or family members. Almost everybody remains anonymous in the book. The exceptions are my mother, with whom I have had many dialogues on the topic of me not choosing to take on the role she says brought her the deepest fulfilment and joy. You will get to know my niece, Stephanie, who, like many of her thirty-something friends, is at the critical point of, "Shall we or shan't we?" In each of the seasons, I have also written about my own journey, or at least how I remember it from the vantage point of my now 64 years. In those chapters, you will meet my partner, Jos, who never for a day in his life has wanted a child.

Throughout the book, you will find quotes from the people who wrote comments in the survey. In order for these to have some context, I have given the gender, age, profession, and country as indicated by these respondents. You will also encounter authors who have already looked into this matter. I have gratefully made use of their research and insights. As always, in the back you will find a list of books I found interesting, useful, and insightful during the course of my explorations into this topic.

In writing this book, I wanted to show that childless living is a viable option, a good choice for a rich life. By no means is it my intention to speak out against having children. Childless living is not for everyone, and heaven forbid that we should all stop bringing new life onto this earth. I do, however, want to promote childless living to those of us around the globe for whom this is our calling—the more of us staying true to ourselves, the better.

Spring

Promise and Potential

That time of year when the farmers plough and sow, the sap begins to flow, and fresh green shoots appear on the trees, flowers push through the surface of the earth to dazzle us with their bright colours, and birds fly by, with twigs and bits to build their nests. These are the years when we are shaped and formed within the confines of our particular family. With a future hidden within us, we leave home as young adults. We move into a world full of possibility and begin to discover who we are and how our life might unfold.

1

The Dilemma

S he has come straight from work, eager to talk to me about the topic of not having children. Not yet for her, she says—maybe later; potentially, never at all. How to decide? How to know what will give true fulfilment in life? How to realize what is meant to be?

I pour tea and let her catch her breath, but she is on a roll.

"A friend of mine has never wanted children, nor has her partner. When they say this out loud in our group of friends, they are met with an icy silence. Those who are trying for children turn away, singles raise their eyebrows, people who just had a baby look offended, and no one really knows how to start the conversation again. Yet I feel some envy, for they seem to have this clear-cut idea of their future. I waver in view of the momentous decision whether or not to have children, because it will colour my life forever."

She takes a small sip and frowns whilst I remain silent, allowing her to think her own thoughts, marvelling at how we can't predict what will arise in another person.

"I think I would love to have the experience of being pregnant," she says eventually, "but with so much to do and to discover, this doesn't really rank high on my priority list. Also, of course, after nine months of pregnancy, there is a lifetime of worry and care about another human being."

She shudders involuntarily, and I am not sure if she notices this physical reaction to her own words, before she continues.

"I wonder if, later in life, I will regret not having children. I also question if I am even capable of having a child and a partner and a job. I don't know how people do it. Can we have it all? I don't think so, to be honest. Yet, wouldn't it be great if we could?"

Having put her cards on the table, she looks at me questioningly, this young woman. Clearly, she wants to hear how I, who have no children, look back on my life, now that children of my friends start to have children of their own.

"I do not envy my friends who become grandparents one bit," I can truthfully say to her. "I just see the whole child circus start over again, and whilst I note my friends' deep pride and joy and begrudge them none of it, not one little smidgen, I am delighted to be able to go my own way, unhampered by granny days."

I pour more tea, always more tea—pu-erh this evening, cultivated high in the mountains of Taiwan, pressed into compact tablets, brought down on muleback, shipped all over the globe, sold in a small shop here in Amsterdam, now fragrant in our cups. I think of the tea farmers and their daughters and sons, who may not have the wide array of choices that the young woman across from me at the kitchen table and I have. They may be destined to marry someone who is willing to toil the land of their forebears and procreate so there will be new hands to pick the leaves.

> "I live in a small town. The impact of being 35 and not having kids in small town America is definitely something we need to start talking about as women. Do I think I would feel more accepted in a more urban area? 100 percent yes."
>
> —Woman, 35, teacher, United States

Across the globe, the freedom to choose what will define our lives is vastly different. We who have many options open to us often suffer from stress, because this freedom brings with it a responsibility of being a good judge of what fits us best. We cannot blame our parents or the system for forcing our hand. The choice about how we lead our lives is up to us, so we had better get it right. At least, this is how it seems.

2

The Inner Film

Another angle is that we do not lead our life, but follow it. Lately, I have been working with the image of an inner film reel. In the old days, when films were not shot digitally but truly on film, they would come in large round tins and be projected at the back of the movie theatre by an operator. In the 1960s, when my young father showed his home movies to us, all ready for bed in our pajamas, the small projector would make a purring sound as the pins passed through the perforations moving the reel along. That was until one got stuck, and before our eyes, the material would melt, and my father would quickly stop the machine, take the film out, cut the damaged piece out and, with lips pursed, glue the two ends together with a special little device. We would sit still, not utter a word, lest he lose his concentration and we our evening entertainment and late bedtime.

Being of that age, I still picture the inner film reel as a band of celluloid with the essential ingredients for our life on it. We bring the images to life when we let the light of our heart shine through like the warm lamp of the projector. The more we are able to open our hearts, the brighter the light can shine and the more colour we are able to bring to our own lives and that of others.

The film reel, however, has a certain width. It is my job to stay within the projected bandwidth. This width defines the scope of who I am meant to be and what I am meant to do. Whenever I stray outside of the projection, I move into the dark. I become irritable, then unhappy, as I grope my way outside the path lit by the lamp of my heart. I don't feel good in my own skin. My energy becomes heavy because I need to manufacture it all myself, now that I am disconnected from the source of my being, the universal life force. I need to get back to centre somehow, back to where the light shines through life as it is meant for me to live.

> "I would love children but not yet. Now I want to enjoy time with my boyfriend and travel, as I have noticed how much a child can change a relationship."
>
> —Woman, 32, PR and communications consultant, the Netherlands

My young friend slowly nods her head when I unfold my metaphor to her. I move my hands in front of my chest to show her the width of my reel.

"My impression is that my film reel is quite narrow," I tell her, meanwhile testing the boundaries with my hands. "Some people have a much broader field that they can play in. They can project out from their heart widely, as if it is a fish eye. They can have children or not have children; it is perfect for them either way. They can accommodate a lot. I never could. I need to stay true to my narrow band of light and follow each next step in my life as it reveals itself. This is what I have learned over the years. This is also how it has become apparent to me in my thirties that a life with children was not for me. To this day, I feel grateful that I have not let my conventional mind nor the expectations of others overrule what was on my inner film."

With her hands she tests the width of her own inner reel. She doesn't think hers is very broad either. She looks at me pensively.

"Leadership is the thing these days," she observes. "I never thought about followership or how to forge a precise path that reflects who I am. I am not sure children are on my film reel. What I want most now is to feel balanced and grateful for who I am."

Finding out who we are is a lifelong endeavour. If we are lucky, we are stimulated to become who we are from childhood. One of my heroes is Maria Montessori. This feisty Italian woman travelled and lectured all over the world about her controversial pedagogy, based

on the conviction that education needs to serve the independence
and innate psychological development of children.

"When a new being comes into existence," she wrote in her 1936
book *The Secret of Childhood*, "it contains within itself mysterious
guiding principles which will be the source of its work, character, and
adaptation to its surroundings."

Her aim was for education to cater to the innate needs and ten-
dencies of a child, so it can grow its potential and become the adult it
is meant to be. I count myself lucky to have attended a Montessori
school for two years as a kindergartener. In those early years, the sense
was instilled in me to trust my intuition and follow it as guidance to
the expression of my innermost being.

Step by step, frame by frame, life reveals itself to us, through us.
An artist friend says he teaches people to build pictures by making
each line as beautiful as they can. This cannot but result in a beautiful
drawing is his stance. If we make each step in our lives as truthful to
who we are as we can, we end up with a life in which we are true to
ourselves.

3

Nieces and Nephews

I am profoundly grateful that my brothers and sister have children, 11 in total. I am not close to the youngest three, who live abroad, but I keep in touch with the others, as they do with me. In their twenties and early thirties now, they are finding their footing in adulthood, and my role of aunt is turning into one of a friend.

Over the years, we revisited the topic of me not having children. "Why didn't you give us playmates, Lie?" they used to ask in the repetitive way of little children. Coming to stay with me for a night or a weekend, they would fantasize about what my children would have looked like and how they would be. In those young years, they themselves had no doubt whatsoever that one day they would have a family similar to the one they came from.

In their teenage years, their views started to differentiate. Whilst one remained utterly convinced that nothing in life would be better than having a large family of her own as soon as possible, others started to voice doubts.

"You can go on holiday when you like," one would observe wisely.

"You can sleep in as long as you like on Sundays," another would quip with adolescent envy.

"You don't need to go grocery shopping all the time," a third would pipe up.

My life wasn't so bad, they agreed. Maybe, just maybe, they would like to remain childless as well. They flirt with the idea now, testing it out, feeling that they still have time, and maybe time will decide for them, at least for my nieces.

With none of them a parent yet, they are in step with the rest of their peers in our part of the world who tend to postpone parenthood. In 2016, using data from *The CIA World Factbook*, UNICEF, and China's Sixth Nationwide Census, a map was made that recorded the average age women become mothers. The ages of first-time mums from 141 countries in the study range from 18 to 31.2 years, with the highest ages being more common in Greece, Australia, South Korea, Japan, Italy, Switzerland, Luxembourg, Singapore, Spain, Hong Kong, Ireland, and my own country, the Netherlands, with an average first-time age of 29.4, closely followed by the other European countries.

The countries with the youngest first-time mothers are Angola, Bangladesh, Niger, Chad, Mali, Guinea, Uganda, Mozambique, and Malawi, with an average age of between 18 and 19 years.

> "I am still in doubt about whether or not to have children, but my partner is convinced that she doesn't want them. We speak about this often, hence my interest in this topic."
>
> —Man, 33, civil servant, the Netherlands

Whilst postponing having children gives women, in particular, a chance to focus on building a strong work base before they embark on a multi-track life of work, children, wiping bottoms and tears, shopping, cooking, washing, setting boundaries, answering life questions, helping with homework, and generally turning little toads into princes and princesses, it brings issues of its own.

On average as women, we are at our most fertile when we are 20. From age 30 onwards, chances to become pregnant are on the decrease, due to having fewer eggs left. With an average 20 percent chance of getting pregnant during each monthly cycle in our thirties, it is also true that our eggs have aged with us and may suffer from chromosomal defects.

Obviously, delaying also affects the number of children a woman might have. You're not going to have 11 children if you start at age 35, unless, of course, through IVF, you have sextuplets and then quintuplets, but goodness, gracious me, I wouldn't wish that on any-body, especially not the babies.

My nieces and nephews know these figures, too. With the opti-mism of youth and the zeitgeist having its way with them, none of them are ready yet for parenthood. They think about the timing. They ponder how to have children outside of a heteronormative rela-tionship. They are still enjoying their freedom. Statistically, the odds are that one or more of them will not have children at all. Social researchers agree that around 20 percent of people now in their repro-ductive years will not have children.

It is not the first time in history that there are so many of us who are childless. In the first half of the 20th century, during the Great Depression and the Second World War, women in industrialized countries delayed motherhood. For a great number of them, this delay turned out to be final, with 20–25 percent of women not becoming mothers. After the war years came the baby boom. Many of us boomers then started the upward trend of childless living that we have seen growing since the 1980s.

When comparing his life choices to mine, my brother says that he had his heart blown open by the birth of each of his four children. He would love for them, too, to experience this depth of love. He grins when he unfolds his theory that as adults we choose like-minded friends. Children, he says, come with unexpected personality traits, firmly held opinions, and challenging choices of their own, which catapult parents out of their comfort zone.

He alleges that he can identify people who have no children in that they are much more set in their ways. He is ready for grandchildren, he says, and our 90-year-old mother chips in that she thinks it is high time she became a great-grandmother.

I try to locate inside myself a desire for the next generation to come skipping along, but cannot identify any longing for my cher-ished nephews and nieces to reproduce. I do, however, register a certain possessiveness in me, a delight that my nieces and nephews are still leading "my kind of life". This is not only about them not being cooped up in a world of nappies and prams and a tight-knit schedule of sitters; it's that I love to have them roam around freely, like me, and for us to be able to spend unimpeded time together. There is another layer, though, that is not so pretty. I like having them, so to speak, in my camp, on my side of the hedge that divides the world into parents and non-parents. I notice how a part of me still wants recognition that my childfree choice is viable and how in the turns and twists of my mind, their delay in starting a family somehow justifies my not doing it at all.

> "I have a severe medical condition that has prevented me from having children. However, when this was discovered, at age 26, instead of being distraught, I was relieved—so relieved that I questioned my desire for motherhood at this young age. I realized that I was not interested at all. Plus, my illness was so painful, and I was so often in hospital, that the idea of being pregnant seemed like having one more disease. Put me off forever."
>
> —Woman, 56, managing director, France

I am being painfully honest here. I would, if I could, recommend childless living to anyone who doubts whether parenthood is for them. Yet, part of me still wants the approval of my family, of society as a whole, which is so easily granted to those who breed.

4

A Positive Choice

"Mummy?"

"Yes, what is it?"

"Babies come from your tummy, don't they?"

"Uh, yes, darling. You and your sister came from my tummy."

"I am never going to have a baby in my tummy."

"You aren't? How can you be so sure?"

"Because I just know that I am not going to be a mum like you."

"Wouldn't you like to be a mum like me?"

"It doesn't matter if I like it or not; I'm just not going to be a mum."

The woman, who is now a diplomat, was four years old when she had this conversation with her mother. She doesn't remember it, but her mother does. When her daughter made one choice after another that led to having a full work load and postings abroad, the mother would smile knowingly and repeat her early words back to her: "I just know that I am not going to be a mum like you."

When the mother had told others of her young daughter's statement, most people had waved it away as child talk.

"She will meet someone and start a family. Just wait and see," they said in an attempt to reassure her, as if that was what she needed. Her mother's eye, however, saw the child for who she was: a determined person who would grow into an ambitious woman who would forge her own path.

This Dutch diplomat belongs to a group that researchers call Early Articulators, those women—about one-third of all women and men without children—who categorically and unequivocally reject the parental role in early life.

In the course of my research, I have met many people who have never felt a desire or instinctual drive to have children. A Dutchman whose source of joy is that he is free to follow wherever his wanderlust takes him. A Dutch woman, part-time photographer, part-time responsible for the real estate her family's company owns internationally, who never had the inclination to be full-time responsible for kids. An Egyptian thirty-something entrepreneur who prefers starting new projects to create jobs for women over the trappings of married life and children. A Canadian who has chosen to live like a monk in the interests of devoting himself to the evolution of human potential. A young Dutch woman, potentially our country's next wine master, who loves the flow in her life. She often comes home late from tastings or spontaneously brings friends home for dinner and rejoices in having a partner who does the same. Another Dutch woman who loves to be by herself and rebels against the notion that, because she happens to have no children, she should make a huge career. A Norwegian who wears her female body like a garment that doesn't define her identity and who cannot remember ever having had the slightest interest in children of others, let alone her own. Men and women who say there are enough children in the world to care for without bringing any extra into the game. Couples who shied away from having a family, because they felt they would have loved them so much, that it would not have been good either for them or their children.

I ran into a group of Taiwanese students sent overseas to study best practices in sustainability in other countries. They giggle, with their hands quickly put in front of their mouths, when I suggest that a fast route to sustainability is not having children. There is no word for childlessness in Mandarin or Taiwanese, they tell me, because this phenomenon is non-existent in their culture. I claim that infertility certainly cannot have bypassed their 23.5 million population. They shake their heads. They know no adult who is not a parent. When I ask about how they see their own life in this respect, they get so excited that they start to talk amongst themselves in Taiwanese. Finally, a young woman tells me that of all of them, she is the only one who doesn't want children. "But," she says, "I am not sure if I can do that. There will be much pressure."

Being an eldest daughter, I certainly felt pressure to marry and have children. My mother, bless her, just could not imagine what could be more fulfilling than being a spouse and having a family. I am part of that wave of boomers who denounced our mothers' 1950s housewife lives by proclaiming that such a measure of service surely wasn't what womanhood was about. We wanted to be free to fulfil our potential. We wanted to be financially self-sufficient and, whilst some of us were able seemingly to do it all, those of us with a narrower band-width opted for a life without children.

Even as my student friends and I were discussing all of the above late into the night, unbeknownst to us an attempt to introduce the word *pronatalism* into the general vocabulary was being made by the editors of the 1974 book *Pronatalism: The Myth of Mom & Apple Pie,* a compilation featuring contributions from scientists, journalists, and role models.

Their introduction states: "A key element in pronatalist thought is the age-old idea that woman's role must involve maternity—that woman's destiny and fulfilment are closely wedded to the *natal,* or birth, experience. Simply and literally, pronatalism refers to any attitude or policy that is 'pro-birth', that encourages reproduction, that exalts the role of parenthood."

The editors, Ellen Peck and Judith Senderowitz, wanted to show that we are all subject to scores of unseen pressures and hidden forces that urge young people to have babies, regardless of personal preference or even competence. They argue that motives for parenthood aren't universal. Not everyone wants to become a parent, not everyone should. The decision is up to the individual, and whether they choose to procreate or not should be greeted with an equal amount of interest and enthusiasm. They fulminate against the litany repeated throughout childhood, "When you have children of your own. . ." stating that replacing *when* by *if* would make all the difference.

"I finally got my salpingectomy [surgical removal of a fallopian tube], and I'm really happy. Children aren't for me. In Italy, it is really difficult to find a doctor who will agree to give you permanent birth control if you don't have any children, but after years of fighting I made it, and it's a great goal for me."

—Woman, 34, dog groomer, Italy

Fast-forward almost half a century and the "when-to/if" issue is still just as relevant, as signalled by essayist, performance poet, and social justice advocate Christen Reighter.

In her 2016 TEDx Talk entitled, "I Don't Want Children. Stop Telling Me to Change My Mind," Christen Reighter talks about her choice to become surgically sterilized. Texan by birth, she realized at a young age that women were not only supposed to have children but to want them, too. She didn't. Reading up on the existing information only confirmed her inner knowing.

When she met all of the legal requirements to have preventive surgery in her state—to be 21 years old, act of her own accord, be of sound mind, and observe a 30-day waiting period—this young woman was baffled by the fact that she still had to battle for what she wanted. She told the doctor about her research, her relationship, and how this decision was integral to who she was. He only wanted to know how her partner felt. She told him that she was aware that biology is only one way to have a family, and that she saw other ways to proceed should she ever come to regret her decision.

The doctor would not approve the procedure, and told her no one else would, either. She heard him describe her to a colleague in the hallway as "a little girl" and allowed herself to be belittled, since this was her one shot at getting the procedure done. She had not, she says in her soft-spoken way, been aware of how strongly society clings to the role of women as mothers. She had always believed that having children was an extension of womanhood, not the definition of it.

"When we say a woman's purpose is to create life, we say her entire existence is a means to an end," she says as she wraps up her talk, which has been viewed almost half a million times online. "There are many paths to fulfilment, and they all look very different. I want women to know that their choice to embrace or forego motherhood is not in any way tied to their worthiness. There absolutely is a choice, and it is yours, and yours alone."

In the United Kingdom, Holly Brockwell published a column in the *Daily Mail* about her four-year fight with the National Health Service for the right to be sterilized. She was 26 when she first requested to have "her tubes tied". After the operation, she writes about how euphoric she feels, finally knowing that she won't have an unwanted pregnancy. "I've been patronized, ignored, harassed, judged, and demonized, but I've never wavered in my determination to be sterilized."

Those who are more extreme and more vocal, as always, get the floor. Yet, these women are spearheading a trend of wanting to exercise control over their lives by making sure pregnancy doesn't happen to them in the heat of the moment. On the website Huffington Post and member forums like The Childfree Life, twenty-somethings bitterly and bitingly write about being rebuffed.

The American College of Obstetricians and Gynecologists (ACOG) recently updated its policy on sterilization, stating that it is both a safe and effective means of permanent birth control. "Women who have completed their childbearing are candidates for sterilization," the policy reads, without specifying whether this includes young women who are convinced they've completed before having begun. Research carried out by the college in 2008 indicates that up to 26 percent of female patients say that they later regret the procedure. Women who were under 30 when sterilized were found to be twice as likely as their older counterparts to say they had misgivings later.

Ultimately, ACOG's official stance is that, whatever her age, if a woman is well informed and seeks sterilization, she should be made aware of the factors that have been shown to increase the risk of subsequent regret, but in the end, the decision is hers.

"For some young women who don't want to have children," Catherine Pearson writes in the Huffington Post in December 2017, "irreversibility is exactly what they are looking for."

In an article on the website Offbeat Home & Life, Heather Gentry talks about why she had tubal ligation before she turned 30. She went to see her gynaecologist for permanent, non-hormonal birth control. Having tried to decide between a temporary intrauterine device and a permanent spring, she was floored when the doctor suggested getting her tubes tied. ("They'll put you to sleep, then you'll wake up and it will be over. There is minimal pain, because it is a laparoscopic procedure.")

Heather Gentry didn't take the decision to have surgery lightly. She wrote in her journal; she talked to her husband; she talked to herself. When she had made up her mind to do it, telling other people only served to confirm her in her course of action. For her, the question was never, "Do I want children?" The question was always, "Do I want to have the surgery?"

When I speak about my research to a neighbour, it turns out she already had the same operation back in 1974, when she was 27. She was married. She also had a lover and didn't want to run the risk of becoming pregnant by either one of them. She is crazy about children, she says, and that is why she didn't want any. She has always made sure that she had young people in her life, children of friends, children she babysat. She has never regretted her decision to take matters into her own hands.

"The purpose of life is our life," this 70-year-old wise woman says. "It has taken me a while to get to this philosophical stance, because initially I thought we had to do something, but that isn't so. All we need to do is be who we are and give as much love as we can."

Despite the fact that books and articles tend to concentrate on the women's perspective on life without children, the issue is not exclusive to this gender, of course. On social media, men also talk about their own choice to be sterilized and speak out in support of women advocating for themselves.

"I'm a guy, and I encountered the same issue," writes one man in response to Christen Reighter.

Another man notes, "My girlfriend and I don't want children, and it's always the same conversation: you'll change your mind, you're selfish, you're not a man, she's not a woman." And another one says, "I'm a guy and also don't want kids. That's a responsible decision for some people, and more people should accept that."

"I'm happy it's becoming less strange to not have children. People have always thought I couldn't have them, though it's a very conscious choice, and people always told me I'll regret it, but so far, nope. It's becoming a bit less weird to not follow what society expects, and I'm happy with that. I finally don't have to 'defend' myself for not over-populating the world."

—Woman, 36, content manager, the Netherlands

One woman who always knew that she wasn't mother material is Tunesian Hayyet Tabboui.

She writes: "When I was a child, we would sit with my cousins at my grandmother's house, all girls. Once, I must have been five or six years old, she asked, 'How many children will you have when you get married?' My cousins replied, 'I want five children!' 'I want three!' 'I want four!' I simply said, 'Zero.' They were all shocked, but I explained that there were already a lot of children. Since then I felt I don't want children, even if I love my nieces and nephews and all the children I see. For me it was a very natural choice."

At age 36, Hayyet Tabboui is the founder of Sidi Bouzitoun, which promotes ecotourism and nature preservation, especially old trees. The association's members meet under a centuries-old olive tree.

"Now when I tell my grandmother about women like me who don't want to have children, she says that each one is a *mara'a w nuss*—a woman and a half—acknowledging our strength to take such a position and make choices in our lives."

If there is *pro*natalism, there is also *anti*natalism, as Reem Khokhar, 38, married and childless by choice, recently discovered. On Scroll.in, which as an independent news venture focuses on political and cultural stories that shape contemporary India, Reem Khokhar describes antinatalism as "a philosophy that believes it's cruel to bring humans into this overburdened world".

Radical antinatalists view birth as morally wrong because it prolongs human suffering, and no one should do that. More moderate believers are not set on keeping everyone on the planet from procreating but wish to slow down population growth through their own abstinence.

With its 1.3 billion people, India is the world's second most populous country which, if birth rates stay as they are, will outrank China by 2024. Environmental problems stemming from overpopulation are rife with, for instance, every third child in Delhi suffering irreversible lung damage due to pollution.

According to Reem Khokhar, environmental concerns inform the decision of a growing number of Indian urbanites to be childfree or, in case they wish to be parents, choose to adopt a homeless orphan. The latter would be her way to go, she says, if unexpected maternal feelings would surface. For now, however, she pleads against cultural pressure to have children and to consider that parenthood doesn't need to be part of everyone's journey unless they really want it.

5

Head, Heart, and Hormones

Travelling alongside those who have always known children were not in their life plan are those who are inclined this way one day and that way the next. Some of them decide to let nature take its course.

"If children come, they are welcome. If they don't, then we will also have a good life together," says a 27-year old hairdresser and make-up artist whose family, like that of her husband's, hails from Afghanistan.

I talk to people beyond child-bearing years who have used this spontaneous approach. Mostly, I notice on the basis of my non-scientific probes, these couples are immensely happy together. Children would have enriched their lives, they think, and they are grateful for the freedom they enjoy, the options that have remained open to them, the way they have been able to shape their existence based on their own preferences.

In another category are those who haven't decided yet and are not sure how on earth this decision is even arrived at.

"I am utterly undecided," my 33-year-old niece Stephanie says, flashing her characteristic quick smile. Her best friends are suddenly pregnant and giving birth. She witnesses some of them dive fully into motherhood, with others remaining more accessible to her as a friend. She herself is happy with her partner of a decade, and whilst she would love to experience the phenomenon of pregnancy, she is building her business and embarking on a new master's degree.

"I am permanently trying to carve out more time for myself. He is invariably busy on projects, if he is not working. We both love to spend time with family and friends. I don't see how we could fit a child into the mix," she laughs.

In a nutshell, this is the dilemma of young urbanites all over the globe now that the days of growing up, hitching up, and starting a family without giving it a second thought are behind us. The trouble is that thinking about this irrevocable life decision doesn't provide an easy answer.

Who in their right mind would ever start having children? Who would voluntarily open themselves to a love so profound that from one moment to the next our well-being depends on the health and happiness of a tiny other person? Who would voluntarily sign up for long years of unpaid caring and ceaseless worrying without any guarantee of being loved back or even appreciated? Who would be willing to give up their free time for the benefit of a next generation, when they could have all the time, energy, and freedom to live a full life of their own?

Who would? Hundreds of thousands do it every day of the week. Yet, when we are not sure if this is the way for us, how on earth do we get to the point where head, heart, and hormones agree on which course to chart for the rest of our life?

Musing about having a baby is not just about the child. It is, in fact, pondering the whole of life as we are going to live it, the roles we will fulfil, the qualities we will develop and the ones we will not.

"Who will I become?" was a question best-selling author Naomi Wolf entertained when she found out she was with child. And, "How will I not only give birth but also become a mother?"

Through conversations with friends and interviews with peers, she became aware that giving birth is intrinsically linked with symbolic deaths, which is not mentioned in upbeat books about motherhood, such as the popular *What to Expect When You're Expecting*. In her 2001 book *Misconceptions: Truth, Lies, and the Unexpected on the Journey to Motherhood*, Naomi Wolf names these deaths as, "the end of her solitary selfhood, the loss of her prematernal shape, the eclipse of her psychologically carefree identity, the transformation of her marriage, and the decline in her status as a professional or a worker."

What she found was that only in intimate conversations will women speak of missing and mourning their old existence and previous identity. Most do it in silence and whisper only of this to friends they trust with their life.

The author has been met with the criticism that she and the women she interviewed were "whining". Here she retorts, "If complaining about something that is difficult or taxing, or expressing fatigue, loneliness, or sadness, or even at times feeling overwhelmed and sorry for oneself and saying so, is 'whining', we are certainly sometimes doing that."

She goes on to say that, having invited negative as well as positive emotions in her interviews with pregnant women and new mothers, she, too, was taken by surprise by the sense of loss she encountered. "I could not stop the well of complaints from overflowing," she writes. "And these were sane, stable, loving, reasonably well-adjusted women who loved their children and their men."

> "Not having children for me has nothing to do with circumstances, life partners, or family. I already spoke about not wanting children with my mother, who had six. She fully understood, while she herself had not had a choice."
>
> —Woman, 56, entrepreneur and creative strategist, the Netherlands

Psychologist Diane Polnow compares bringing another person into this world to purchasing a one-way, non-stop ticket for the longest, most unpredictable, and most important flight of a lifetime. "There are no refunds," she writes in her 2012 book *Baby Debate*, "no cancellations, no do-overs, and there is no turning back once you've departed."

When she was seven, she came home from school one day with the assignment to draw a family tree. Her dad sat her and her older brother down and broke the news that they were both adopted. She remembers feeling betrayed that the people she had trusted unconditionally had been lying to her all along. When attempts to meet her birth mother resulted only in being snubbed, she found her life's mission.

Knowing the hurt and pain she had experienced as a result of having been given up by her birth mother, she decided to help prospective parents make an informed decision and look beyond the adorable baby stage before making this huge life commitment. Methodically, she addresses all aspects of what it takes to have a baby and raise it into adulthood. Part of her reality check is relentlessly adding up the costs of housing, transportation, food, clothing, healthcare, and education involved in child rearing. Including miscellaneous expenses, she comes to a whopping half a million dollars. This somewhat staggering amount still doesn't include costs of maternity and/or paternity leave, furnishing, a bigger car, holidays, and extracurricular activities.

Continuing to burst the bubble of idealized concepts around having a baby, she also addresses the strength of the relationship and the question of whether both partners are clear on the role they do and do not want to play in the life of their offspring. For those who are not sure, she also suggests that taking on a pet first might do the trick. Diane Polnow's rational approach might not be everybody's cup of tea, but she does have a point: entering into the lifelong commitment of being a parent is better done on the basis of some soul-searching into one's destiny and an understanding of what it takes.

Hormones also play a considerable part, of course. Some of us who have no children confirm that we have never experienced the onset of these determining chemical substances, which make us view life and what we want 180 degrees differently from just a second ago. I have seen friends turn broody from one instant to the next. They wanted a baby, and they had to have it now. They threw their remaining stack of pills and condoms in the bin. They found a partner, if they didn't have one. They did whatever it took, as there is no reasoning with that commanding force of nature once it starts to happen. Evolution is very persuasive in wanting to take care of itself into the future.

The upper age limit for when it was deemed both medically possible and socially acceptable to become a first-time mum somehow grew higher as I myself aged. When I was in my twenties, the medical advice was to have your first child before age 30. When I turned 30, the limit had somehow been raised to 32; mysteriously it then became 35, then 39. I have two friends who, after meeting their partners late in life, had their first child at age 44. An American woman of 47 tells me that the pregnancies of two cousins recently led her to revisit her decision not to have children, given that one cousin is 49, the other 50, and both have just had their first child.

When I tell her this, my niece Stephanie shudders at the idea of having this life-determining question hang over her head for another 15 years. Her partner has just come up with another argument in favour of them starting a family, "When you are away, I will at least have a little version of you around." She wrinkles her nose when she shares this endearing reason with me.

I give her the recommendation from one of the childfree couples Laura Carroll interviewed for her book *Families of Two*. When asked for any advice she could share with a couple trying to decide about a future with children, one of her respondents, Carla, said "I would tell them to do the 'death bed test'. I imagine myself 97 years old, in a rest home, lying there dying, and thinking back over my life. I would recommend they ask themselves: 'On my deathbed, will I wish I never had kids, or wish that I had?'"

I go back to the inner film reel. Do you feel that children are an integral part of the life you are meant to live? I believe that deep down we know what is ours to do. We might not want to know. Conditioning and expectations from others, society, and our own may cloud our view. Yet, if we are true to ourselves, we will know whether children are for us or not, and whether we have enough bandwidth to welcome them with open arms, if they come, and be utterly fulfilled, if they don't.

6

My Spring

I was born in 1954, a mere nine years after the end of the Second World War, which impacted the two young people who would become my parents. My mother had grown up a single child in Indonesia, which was a Dutch colony at the time. Her father worked on a tea plantation owned by an English firm. One day he was handed his notice and one of the owners' sons was installed in his stead. The family moved to Jakarta, then called Batavia, where my grandmother became a French teacher in a high school. My grandfather died, and my grandmother remarried soon after.

In 1941, the Japanese invaded Indonesia, overturned the Dutch, and imprisoned them in camps. Without her stepfather, who was transported to an unknown location elsewhere, my mother and her mother moved from one camp to another, trying to find the best place for themselves and their friends to survive.

When the war was over, the Indonesian people, of course, assumed the right to self-governance. This was a dangerous time for the Dutch. By good fortune, one day, my mother's stepfather walked into the camp, exhausted but unharmed. The three of them shipped out to the Netherlands with nothing but the clothes they wore, distributed to them by the Red Cross. In high school, I often wore a big burgundy sweater my mother said must have been knitted by a kind American lady in an effort to ease the plight of people like herself, a DP or Displaced Person.

"My conditioning was 'Grow up, get married, and have kids', and I thought that would be what I would do, even though I didn't know if it was what I wanted. I developed a medical condition in my late twenties that made it difficult but not impossible to carry to full term. Plus by the time I met a partner that I would have considered having kids with, I was too old and set in my non-kid life."

—Woman, 53, doctor of Psychology, Ireland

Once in the Netherlands, they were taken in by my grandmother's sister, to whom she had always been close. The war had taken its toll in Europe, with the winter of 1944 having been especially cold and dubbed "the hunger winter". The Dutch were not interested in the stories of those who came from a warmer climate, so my mother gritted her teeth, showed her gratitude, and finished the years of high school she had missed.

She went on to study English and became part of a student club, where she served on the committee that organized the annual ball. When it came time to make seating arrangements, she insisted on being next to Albert Schuitemaker, although she did not know him. To this day she can picture in her mind's eye how he came in wearing his military uniform. He reached to his back pocket to take out his wallet, and she fell in love.

We have two black-and-white pictures from that first evening they met: my mother is talking in a lively way and my father is looking at her with an expression that seems to say, "Who is this vivacious phenomenon?" As an able-bodied young man, he had spent part of the war years in hiding with a family of religious farmers up north to avoid being drafted to work in the German factories. The two of them got engaged, got married, and a neat two years later, they were delighted to have me..

After the atrocities of the war, my parents were fired up to be part of reconstructing society and making it better. If it was up to them, never again would dictatorship feed on poverty, hunger, and ignorance. Having obtained a degree in economics, my father found employment with a family company, which he would help grow into a worldwide conglomerate.

When my brother was born two years after me, we moved from a small city apartment to a house in a suburb. My sister arrived two years later, and six years on, our youngest brother completed our family. My father pursued a career, whilst my mother took care of us. She cleaned, cooked, and organized our birthday parties. Life was quiet in our suburb, with only women and children on the streets during the day, except for the milkman, who delivered milk to our doorstep, and a handful of teachers, doctors, and the school principal.

Around age 16, my life began to change. I got contact lenses, became a vegetarian, and joined a more alternative group of friends. We listened to music. We spoke about the games people play. And we thought that our lives should be different from the regulated ones of our parents.

After graduating from high school, I spent a lonely year in Brussels studying to be an interpreter. The following year, I was happy to join a student club in Leiden, where I began to study the Classics. Much of what happened in the world passed me by in those years, for the simple reason that my friends and I were fully occupied with our social life, our parties, our attempts at finding a partner for life.

Most of my friends succeeded in doing the latter. I, too, got engaged at some point to a kind man who played the bass in a band, but was otherwise on his way to following in his father's diplomatic footsteps. We didn't really address it, as far as I remember, but I feel it was understood that he would make the career and I would tend to the babies and maybe, if I could wing it, do some work on the side. I pictured myself waving him goodbye in the morning. Even now when I write this, involuntarily I sigh when the image looms again of having to go back into the house, with the children having smeared their breakfast over themselves, the table, and the floor, and somehow managing to get through that day without losing my patience and my mind.

I modelled this notion on the life of my fiancé's sister. I hoped we would, like her, be able to secure a house on the corner, so I could at least have a bit of a view other than the identical family houses across the street. As much as I adored my fiancé's nephews and nieces and loved to babysit them, nothing in me looked forward to that housebound existence.

Then I had a dream. I dreamt that, dressed in gorgeous white, I was led to the altar by my father to find my fiancé waiting. I smiled at him, but when the question was popped, if I would take this man to be my lawfully wedded husband, I said, "No," and heard the full church gasp behind me. When I had the dream again, I broke the engagement as well as this good man's astonished heart.

About one year later, I read an article in a woman's magazine I had borrowed from my mother about three young women who each ran their own companies doing communications and PR. My heart jumped out of my chest. That was what I wanted, too: a free life, a working life, a creative life like I had not seen anyone in my surroundings have. No children, but a company. No house on the corner in a suburb, but a studio apartment in Amsterdam. I had no idea how to go about fashioning such an existence for myself. I knew no one who had done so.

7

Wanting a Different Life

I ponder if choosing not to do something is as major a decision as choosing to do it. Is diving in and going for a swim somehow a bigger choice than staying standing safely by the seashore? Maybe it is—depends on the weather. Is saying yes to another last drink in the bar a stronger choice than declining to do so and risk being called a spoilsport? Probably not.

These might be false comparisons, but when I am completely honest with myself, I do think the choice to go forth and procreate is a bigger one than to refrain from the whole child endeavour. However, deciding to step out of the mainstream does require a certain amount of courage that is not always acknowledged, let alone celebrated.

We all know there is no one-size-fits-all recipe for a good life, and around the world people are speaking up for their choice of a life of their own. The number of young people who embrace the concept of DINK (Double Income No Kids) is rising in China, the *Shanghai Star* reported some time ago. In Hong Kong, according to the *South China Morning Post*, more and more women choose to fly solo, because they are confident in themselves and happy with their professional and personal lives. This paper also reports on the growing success of women in China's business world, and that there are laws to protect women who are pregnant or new mothers but none for single women who contribute just as much to the economy and society as a whole.

"The future of the world economy lies increasingly in the hands of women, and many of them are single, ambitious, career-driven individuals," writes Luisa Tam in her article "Single, Childless, and Maligned". "Women, single or not, should start talking about the issue and make others aware of this unfair perception and treatment. Women should stand up for each other."

When Maxine Trump (who declares herself no relation of the current U.S. president) decided to live childfree, she felt constantly berated by people who "knew better". She looked for books and documentaries, "something to help me, guide me, support me, make me laugh, make me cry". Not finding what she sought, as an award-winning filmmaker she decided to produce what she felt was lacking in the conversation about not wanting to have a family.

Her documentary *To Kid or Not to Kid*, that she has been working on since 2012, premiered to great acclaim in November 2018. The trailer shows a woman at a party sitting on a yellow sofa. People get up to talk to other parents, once they find out she isn't one. A young father sits down to tell her she will get over it, and an older woman wonders if she's ever thought of being ancient and needing offspring to come and visit or care.

The scenes are funny in their dreadful trueness. They transport me back instantly to experiences years ago, when people at dinner parties turned away after I had replied "None" to their question how many children I had. A friend of mine has been pregnant once, suffered an early miscarriage, and never conceived again, She tells me how, in her thirties, she was cold-shouldered by women at a friend's birthday when it turned out she had no children.

Groups can be incredibly harsh when they shield themselves from those who are built to different specifications. Even, or maybe especially, groups of doting mothers can shoot us a quizzical look and resume their conversation as if we don't exist, we with our different lives.

With her film, Maxine Trump wants to show, "Look, we're cool, we're fun, we're caring, we aren't these child-hating witches. We are actually normal, healthy, integrated people, and we might just live next door!"

That wasn't the only reason, though, to embark on the project. She feels that she has got off lightly. Her mother was upset but tried her best to understand her daughter, and the two stayed close. She found many others, however, who have suffered real consequences from their "coming out": disinherited from their families, told that they aren't "real" women, forced to move away from their homes, sacked from their jobs.

In her research, she also spoke to women—especially in less urbanized or cosmopolitan areas—who never realized that they even had a reproductive choice. She is making this film for them, too, for those who are not aware that they have a choice in the first place.

"One woman took me back to the moment when it fully dawned on her that she herself had the power to make this most elemental choice, of whether to have children or not, and that it was okay if she opted out of being a mother. She isn't the exception. Many women can come to recognize these choices once this topic becomes the talking point it should be in our culture."

> "As an introvert and a workaholic, I wouldn't be able to manage with kids in the same way. As a single woman with no children, I feel I am an important example of other life paths and how 'non-traditional' options are just as valid."
>
> —Woman, 45, non-profit administrator and fundraiser, United States

In my own home on a quiet Sunday afternoon, I sit with a young couple. She is a long-time friend of one of my nephews. We have seen each other intermittently for two decades or so and always felt affection. She and her partner are in their late twenties, and to kid or not to kid is an ongoing topic of conversation.

"You would make a great father," friends tell him, when he says that he would rather spend time with like-minded people, thinkers or writers, even if they are dead. He considers it unchallenged selfishness to put yet another child on this overcrowded planet and subsequently hang your happiness on its shoulders.

"Just you wait," they tell him, "one day soon you are going to wish for a mini-me." Meanwhile he couldn't be more convinced that he wants to pursue his own curiosity unhindered and has gone to find out about being sterilized.

She smiles with loving eyes, as he unfolds his resolute vision for their future. Her own mother died young, and with her father focused on his work, the only person she truly found a warm welcome with was an aunt who had no children. At a tender age, she decided that a child should not be put through such loss and grief and loneliness. Now that she has love to give in spades, she is in two minds about her youthful decision. She loves being alone, and yet she is afraid to be lonely. She needs ample time to herself to meditate and do yoga and realizes all too well how much care a child requires every minute of the day.

"No man wants a child. That is up to you to decide," friends assert to her dismay. She would not want to have a child with someone unless he wanted it for the full 100 percent, too. She thinks having children is romanticized. Children gobble up all the attention. And yet she also feels that it would be a pity not to have that experience. Thus, she remains ambivalent.

They still have time to find their common truth, these wise young people who are so open to each other and to me. He, with his vision of uncharted territory that they can form and shape together and with his concern that she will have regrets when the option of having a child is no longer there. She, with her philosophical stance that every human being lives in mourning for the path not walked. She wants a good life with him, she says, and they agree that it will be hard truly to be in relationship with the distraction of children.

I come back to the inner film reel. In some of us, a more unconventional life is imprinted on our inner reel, and it takes time for us to come to grips with that. A good friend who runs her own spiritual coaching school has always carried an image of herself at the head of an unruly table full of kids. She has never found a partner whom she fully recognizes as such and is still in a process of reconciliation with this hand that has been dealt to her—if it is a hand, and if there is a dealer.

She and I talk a lot about God. About how the concept of someone up there who monitors our existence doesn't work for us, because it instantly turns us into children who then start to protest our fate. Could he not have fashioned the world better, made sure there was not so much strife and pain? We conclude there is no god but God. In other words, there is only the One that presents itself as the many, and in the many has the experience of everything all at once.

Apparently, through the two of us, this life without children wanted to be lived, this life without the dictates that family brings, this life of freedom to pursue our curiosity, our interests, our potential. Who wouldn't want such a life, we agree, and yet, whereas I am filled with joy in having followed in my own footsteps, I feel her hesitate. She has cherished her motherly image for so long, held it so dear to her heart, she is still, like my young friend said, in mourning. Maybe her mothering wish was bigger than mine and I got away relatively lightly.

8

The Parental Scale

We don't all have the same mothering or fathering desire in us. Some of us are born to be parents, whilst others are not at all interested. Looking around in our circles of family and friends, colleagues and acquaintances, we can see how true this is. The idea that parenting is not an innate, all-encompassing wish was already upheld by Leta Hollingworth, PhD, in her 1916 article on the topic in the American *Journal of Sociology*.

Born in 1886, this early psychologist had expected to continue teaching in New York, where she had moved with her husband after their wedding. At the time, however, this great city had a policy of prohibiting married women from teaching. Finding homemaking not nearly enough to keep her occupied, she continued her studies.

The concept of maternal instinct had figured prominently in scientific theories since the time of Charles Darwin. In the late 1800s, experts had posited that maternal instinct was located in the female reproductive organs. In Leta Hollingworth's day, it was normal to call any woman who didn't desire offspring abnormal and not womanly. Sterility in "the wife" could be made a cause of divorce. Sharing information about birth control was forbidden.

This upcoming academic came to the conclusion that society silently conscripted women into having children out of the conviction that the next generation is necessary for tribal or national existence. She pointed at the law as a powerful instrument for the control of women. She accused art, with all of its images of madonnas, of promoting the ideal of motherhood without giving enough due to the pain and sacrifice involved.

"There is a strong and fervid insistence on the 'maternal instinct', which is popularly supposed to characterize all women equally, and to furnish them with an all-consuming desire for parenthood, regardless of the personal pain, sacrifice, and disadvantage involved, but there are no verifiable data," she wrote in her article of a century ago. "Since we possess no scientific data at all, it is most reasonable to assume that if it were possible to obtain a quantitative measurement of maternal instinct, we should obtain a curve of distribution, varying from an extreme where individuals have a zero or negative interest in caring for infants, through a mode where there is a moderate amount of impulse to such duties, to an extreme where the only vocational or personal interest lies in maternal activities."

> "My partner never wanted kids, and later I was clear that I, too, did not want kids (even adopted), as I wanted to work on the purpose of my life rather than getting carried away with duties and attachments towards my family."
>
> —Woman, 44, on a journey to find the real meaning of life, India

In other words, with those having no maternal feelings at all on one end of the scale and those born to be a parent at the other, many of us will sit somewhere in between.

When baby-making was still an option, I used to describe myself as a 70/30 person to friends and others who asked if I had children and then wondered why not. I felt that 70 percent of me wanted a different life from the one I had seen my mother and her friends lead and that most of my friends were embarking on. Yet, there was also a part of me that would have loved having a baby grow inside me, delivering it, and having it still bloody and wet and greasy laid on my breast, watching it grow from my own milk, start to coo and grab its own feet, begin to walk and talk, and walk away from me through all the phases of childhood and adolescence, with me there to dry tears, talk sense, and cuddle away heartbreaks. I estimated that 30 percent of me did want this irreplaceable intimacy of mother and child, the bond that is forever through the inevitable ups and downs, this particular kind of love.

I realize that over the years my 70/30 division has shifted. The initial 70 percent of wanting a different life has grown. Looking back, I register only a few slight traces of envy, of a sense of missing out, of feeling excluded from the club of parents and children. I realize that I have now become a 95/5 person. I am delighted with my childless life and don't crave grandchildren that I will never have, even if I see how much joy they bring to my parenting friends.

Talking about this with a friend my age who is also utterly content with her childfree existence, she confesses that she still would love to take every new-born she sees home with her. I also know a woman in her mid-sixties, who is still so pained by the fact that she has remained childless that she crosses the street when she sees someone with a baby come her way. She never sends presents to new parents as she cannot bear to walk into a baby store. She hasn't been able to bring herself to call on her favourite nephew, his wife, and their new-born. Others tell me that they never wanted children, until they themselves had healed from their own harsh childhoods and then they were past childbearing years. We all must find our way with the place we occupy on the parenting scale, with our past and our particular life purpose, which might not be always in line with our personal preference.

9
Sign of the Times

I n her TEDx Talk, Christen Reighter is convincing when she states that the choice about whether or not to have a child is ours, and ours alone; however, this is not the whole truth. The highly personal decision about whether or not to have a child is not one of individuals alone.

For starters, we are all parts of families, traditions, and cultures that make us and our predilections products of the times and the circumstances we are born into. Our choices are informed by the viewpoints we are raised to adopt, even if we, being the next generation to push the envelope, reject them. Another factor is that when whole cohorts of people decide to postpone making the choice of whether or not to procreate, this influences everything from the local restaurant business and the tourist industry to the way governments plan for construction of new housing. When a growing number of us don't go for parenthood at all, this impacts how child-centred or family-oriented our society will become.

This is a revolution, a quiet one as Madelyn Cain signalled in her 2001 book *The Childless Revolution*. A late-in-life mother of a daughter herself, she started out writing from the premise that all women want to mother. She had a lot to learn, she confesses towards the end of the book. Interview by interview, woman by woman, story by story, her beliefs were challenged. She liked the childfree and childless women she met. They were vibrant and fulfilled. Walking into their worlds, she found genuine serenity. Their lives were self-directed, not selfish as she had been led to believe.

Before long, she writes, she was no longer asking, "How would I have been without a child?" She wanted to know, "Who would I be if I were free to choose the way I spend my energies?" Lecturing on childlessness to women's studies classes at universities and colleges in the United States, she found students becoming extremely talkative. They were eager to articulate what had clearly been in their minds before.

Madelyn Cain calls childlessness a very big elephant in our collective living room, which is growing every day without anyone wanting to admit that it is there. According to 1999 U.S. Census Bureau figures, 42.2 percent of the adult female American population between the ages of 15 and 44 are childless, she writes, and these women and the childfree option are still treated as if they do not exist.

"Because these women do not conform to traditional roles, their existence is denied and we maintain a negative view of childlessness," she says. "What little knowledge we do have of childless women is based on negative stereotypes, such as the child-hating workaholic. Our personal knowledge of these women who are our neighbours, our co-workers, our sisters, and our best friends may tell us otherwise, but the accepted viewpoint remains cynical."

More recent U.S. Census figures show that in 2014, 47.6 percent of women between the ages of 15 and 44 had never had children. This represents the highest percentage of childless women since the bureau started tracking that data in 1976, when only 10 percent of women hadn't had children by their forties.

My impression is that childless and childfree living has a slightly better reputation in many places now than two decades ago, when Madelyn Cain did her research. At least we have, so to speak, come out of the closet. Celebrities like Oprah Winfrey, Cameron Diaz, Jennifer Aniston, Ricky Gervais, and Ellen DeGeneres have started to speak openly about their lives, and how they do not like to be defined by the fact that they don't have children.

In her 2010 book on the institution of marriage, *Committed*, author Elizabeth Gilbert wrote about her lack of desire for a baby. This had been the breaking point for her first marriage. Now, about to marry again, she discovered that she had never considered the possibility of a lifelong male companion without being expected to have children. She described the "great thrumming relief that we both felt when we discovered that neither one of us was going to coerce the other into parenthood" and how this still sent a pleasant vibrating hum across their life together.

The many readers who follow Elizabeth Gilbert as she bravely and uncompromisingly exposes her life to the public eye know that she has subsequently left this man of her dreams after realizing that she not only loved, but was in love with, her best friend Rayya Elias. For the third time in her life, the author committed, this time in the knowledge that her beloved would soon die of pancreatic cancer.

> "I support people making their own choices as long as they are not harming others in the process. Therefore, I think it's irresponsible to have children who will not be properly provided for."
>
> —Woman, 35, QA tester, United States

Every week almost, people sent me articles on childlessness. Childless living is a hot topic, and that in itself suggests that our days of being a somewhat strange splinter group are not over. We number one-fifth of the population in many rich countries, 15–20 percent of women and a slightly higher proportion of men, and our share is rising. Yet we are a minority, and we will be regarded as such.

It is telling that in July 2017, when *The Economist* published an article on our growing numbers, they titled it "In Defence of the Childless". The esteemed magazine wrote, "Some have medical problems; others do not meet the right person in time; still others decide they do not want children. Falling sperm count in rich countries may play a role, too. Whatever the cause, the attacks on the childless are baseless."

The article cited European heads of state like Germany's Chancellor Angela Merkel, Britain's Prime Minister Teresa May, and France's President Emmanuel Macron, whose adversaries reproached them for their childlessness during election campaigns, arguing that they could not possibly have a true stake in society as they had not invested in the future by having children.

"If non-breeders are selfish," *The Economist* countered, "they have an odd way of showing it."

The magazine went on to defend the childless citing the economic argument: "The childless are more likely to set up charitable foundations than people with children, and much more likely to bequeath money to good causes. According to one American estimate, the mere fact of not having children raises the amount a person leaves to charity by a little over $10,000. The childless are thus a small but useful counterweight to the world's parents, who perpetuate social immobility by passing on their social and economic advantages to their children."

There you have it. We are not selfish, but giving. We have other priorities and other ways to contribute to society.

10

The Birth of the Pill

One of the major developments in my lifetime has been the introduction of a tiny white pill, which, if we take it daily, allows us as women in our fertile years to have sex without a worry in the world and not become pregnant.

To this day, my mother is proud to be a one-man woman, as she calls it with glee. We looked through her old photo albums recently with their black-and-white pictures, two, maybe three, for every occasion. Asking who was who, I found out that she had had quite a few boyfriends before meeting my father.

"But no hanky-panky," she said. "All proper and safe."

I raised my eyebrows at the word safe. "As in not risking pregnancy?"

She frowned at my incomprehension. "As in not risking my reputation!"

I know she feared for my reputation when I was young. "You don't want to be spoilt goods," she used to tell me primly. Thus, I got used to not telling her what I was up to. I never told her that I went on "the pill"—and she never asked.

We are fortunate to live in a time when contraceptives are so easily available. For as long as men and women have been making babies, we have also been trying not to. The ancient Egyptians made vaginal plugs out of crocodile dung. Aristotle recommended cedar oil and frankincense to kill off sperm. Casanova prescribed the use of half a lemon as a cervical cap.

The little hormone pill that millions of women are now taking did not see the light of day until 1960. I learnt all this from the book *The Birth of the Pill* by Jonathan Eig. Masterfully, he tells the story of how four people banded together in the 1950s to give women the means to control their own destiny and enjoy their sexuality free of the usual consequences—just as men have always done.

First and foremost was the formidable Margaret Sanger. Born in 1879, the sixth of 11 children, she was horrified by the poverty and misery of women who kept getting pregnant only to lose many of their offspring to malnutrition and illness. Convinced that women ought to have a right to contraception, she opened her first birth control clinic in Brooklyn in 1916. Her straightforward articles on what she thought every woman ought to know about sex and contraception got her charged with violating obscenity laws.

A further scandal was that she, a mother of three, ran off to Europe, where she met her second husband, the eminent sexual psychologist Henry Ellis. Under his tutelage, she narrowed her grand scheme of wanting to change the face of capitalism, marriage, and organized religion, all in one go. She began to see that if sex was disconnected from childbirth, women would be liberated in ways they had never imagined. Marriage would change. The meaning of family would change. Career and educational opportunities for women would change. In 1950, Margaret Sanger's heart was failing, but she had not given an inch on her life's purpose of gaining equality for women.

Jonathan Eig opens his informative book with her visit to Gregory Goodwin Pincus, called Goody by his friends, the world's leading expert in mammalian reproduction. Early in his career, he had attempted to breed rabbits in a petri dish, using similar technology to what ultimately would lead to in vitro fertilization, or IVF.

Margaret Sanger explained to him that she was looking for an inexpensive, easy-to-use, and completely fool-proof method of contraception, preferably a pill.

"It should be something a woman could swallow every morning with her orange juice or while brushing her teeth, with or without the consent of the man with whom she is sleeping," she stated. "Something that would make sexual intercourse spontaneous, with no forethought of messy fumbling, no sacrifice of pleasure; something that would not affect a woman's fertility if she wished to have children later in life; something that would work everywhere, from the slums of New York to the jungles of Southeast Asia."

Other scientists had turned her down. The technology wasn't there. Thirty states and the U.S. Federal Government still had anti-birth-control laws. Goody Pincus with his genius IQ and dubious reputation started to work on a solution the next day.

Margaret Sanger had a wealthy ally. Katharine Dexter had been one of the first women to graduate with a degree in science from MIT and was a leader in the women's movement before marrying million-aire Stanley McCormick, who was soon diagnosed as schizophrenic. Convinced that hormone treatments could benefit her beloved, Katherine McCormick funded research, while battling for custody of her insane husband. In 1947, after more than 40 years of living in isolation, his mind ravaged by the disease, the heir to the fortune died, leaving his imposing wife free to spend her money and use her expertise to further contraceptive research.

Goody Pincus needed to test the hormone progesterone on women. He approached the pipe-smoking, conservatively attired Catholic physician John Rock, whose work had centred on helping women overcome infertility. He had reportedly recruited 80 "frustrated but valiantly adventuresome" women for an experiment with hormones. The good and widely trusted doctor did not test on rabbits; he did not have the women sign consent forms. That was how experiments were done at the time. Through a trajectory of breakthroughs and setbacks, this valiant foursome managed to create "the pill" that needed no other name.

In May 1960, after approval by the U.S. Food & Drug Administration, pharmaceutical company Searle, which had funded a lot of the research, sent its army of sales representatives out. In 1961, 400,000 women were taking the pill. A year later that number had tripled. In 1967, *Time* magazine put the pill on its cover as "in a mere six years, it has changed and liberated the sex and family life of a large and still growing segment of the U.S. population: eventually, it promises to do the same for much of the world."

Leta Hollingworth had ended her 1916 article on a similar hopeful note. "The time is coming, and is indeed almost at hand, when all the most intelligent women of the community, who are the most desirable child-bearers, will become conscious of the methods of social control. The type of normality will be questioned; the laws will be repealed and changed; enlightenment will prevail; belief will be seen to rest upon dogmas; illusion will fade away and give place to clearness of view; the bugaboos will lose their power to frighten. How will the 'social guardians' induce women to bear a surplus population when all these cheap, effective methods no longer work?"

Whilst it is true that child brides continue to be married off to much older men every day of the week, and in many places LGBTQIA people still need to remain undercover, it is also true that much has changed in the century since Leta Hollingworth wrote her piece and Margaret Sanger opened her birth control clinic. Policies that married women couldn't teach or work in other jobs have gone the way of the typewriter. Laws that a husband could divorce his wife on the grounds of infertility are no longer in place. In many countries, same-sex marriage has been legalized. Leta Hollingworth's hope of enlightenment of a century ago and the liberation of sex and family life foreseen by *Time* magazine half a century ago haven't happened everywhere, but they have happened in some places and everything has to start somewhere.

11

Many Ways of Living

By definition we all come from a family. Ours may have been the traditional one, in which we lived with our father and mother and one or more siblings. Usually, however, families are messy. We may have come from broken homes in which our father left when we were little, or even before we were born, and our mother toiled to give us what she could. We may have had new temporary partners of our parents in our lives, and maybe they stayed. We may have lived with our grandparents or in foster homes. We may have left home early to fend for ourselves.

As much as romance novels and people who pine for the good old days would like us to believe, life doesn't usually fit in neat little boxes of colourful houses on tree-lined streets, with happy families harmoniously gathered for their supper at six. Less and less so, it seems. In the 1950s, when I was growing up, there was still the pretence of this ideal family in our part of the world.

When she reads this, my mother will immediately grab the phone and protest the word pretence. She was blissfully happy as a wife, a housewife, and a mother, she will say. In fact, she will tell me, again, there was no happier time in her life than when we were small and needed her for everything.

I will then say, my goodness, that was a long time ago, and she must have been happy since those days long gone, which she will not deny. But right before we hang up, she will get the last word in.

"I was happy back then; really, really happy with all of you, and you were happy, too."

I will laugh because this conversation between us has been on repeat for many years now, and we remain perplexed by each other's sources of joy and fulfilment.

However, no one can deny the increased variety we see in our societies of ways to live. Cohabitation, to use the official term for two or more people living together without being married, has become common in Western countries.

Although many people might still object to children born out of wedlock, the numbers of couples who go for this option are on the increase. In the United States, for instance, 35.7 percent of the women between the ages of 15 and 50 who gave birth in the year 2015 were not married. We may all know one or more women who have made the choice to have a baby on their own. Add current divorce rates, and so it is that around half of today's mothers will spend at least a few years as the sole custodial parent. At any one time, almost a quarter of mothers are single mothers.

We may know homosexual men and women with children. I know one lesbian couple who had the egg of the one partner, once it was impregnated, planted into the womb of the other, so they could both be parents to their beautiful girl.

I know of more than one couple who had someone over for dinner who stayed the night and didn't leave for the next five years. I know people who live alone and love it.

I know many co-parents who live down the street from one another so that the children don't need to travel far when they change home base. I know children who fly on planes from a young age, sent from one parent to the other.

Someone told me of her upstairs neighbours, a couple where the man is 15 years younger than the woman, who every other weekend have the son of a single mother over, so she can have some time to herself and they get to enjoy being makeshift parents.

I know a man whose wife, mother of his children, to his utter surprise, told him on her deathbed to please find a good man to love, seeing as he still had so much to give. He was astounded that she apparently had been aware of the fact that he was attracted to men rather than women.

I know a couple who, after years of living together and raising their respective offspring, registered to get married and forgot to show up twice.

I know working mothers and stay-at-home fathers, and vice versa.

I know a man who is going to marry for the third time, because this brings peace to the heart of his beloved's daughter by a father who makes only occasional appearances.

I know men and women who have chosen celibacy in order to be fully open to Spirit.

I know women who share a house for companionship as they get along well.

I know women who share a room with their beloved only when the two of them travel abroad, on the grounds that they cannot be seen to do so in their respective countries.

I know traditional couples who marry and have children and negotiate the traffic and remain happy, a good team together.

We come in all sizes, and so do the ways we find to build relationships within the confines of our own likings and those of the society we are born into.

In many countries nowadays, millennials no longer see having children as an obvious choice or an inevitable milestone. They cite many reasons for this rising tide that magazines call a "baby bust" or "the post-familial society".

Financial instability is prominent in their considerations. With a student loan to be paid back and the job market tight, they don't deem it wise to add the cost of a baby to their precarious financial situation.

Science also plays a role now that many are aware of genetic disorders that we might pass on to the next generation, whilst our ancestors did so in blessed ignorance. Some feel it is better not to have a child, whilst still recovering from a childhood with dysfunctional parents who were not up to the task. Also, many don't want to replicate their parents' harmful behaviours. Some cite their own health or mental issues.

A good many are deterred by the risks of pregnancy itself. My niece Nina tells me of a friend who might want a child one day but has told her partner that she is not having it come from her womb. The official term for this, *tokophobia*, is new to me, but if there is a word, this woman will not be the only one who abhors having a child grow inside her.

With hurricanes, fires, and floods as a result of climate change, a growing number of youngsters don't want to contribute to the over-population and overconsumption by adding a child of their own. Some feel the world is a scary place, and they are terrified of raising a child to be a good human in it and keeping them safe. Others opt for career goals. Some just don't want children. Period. We may like them, but we also really like to leave them with their parents and go back to our own quiet haven, where we can have uninterrupted conversations about grown-up topics.

Whilst this choice is not open to all of us around the globe, it is open to many, and the conversation about whether or not isn't as exotic as it used to be. Childless living is just one of the ingredients that add spice to societies.

12

No Reasons Needed

Posting on a Dutch Facebook group called "Sisters", which has over 16,000 members, a young woman started a conversation about making the choice to have a child. She was still in the process of making up her mind, she wrote, and wondered how others had reached their decisions.

Within hours, hundreds of women had posted their reactions.

Some of the responders talked about their unhappy childhoods and how they wanted to heal and transform traumas that had been running in their families for generations. Others wrote about how long it had taken them to get themselves and their lives together, to gain some sort of inner ground and begin to love themselves. Some spoke of the way they have always cherished time with themselves and how they made the choice to honour that need.

One woman wrote that the word childless didn't resonate with her at all, because it implied she was lacking something. "Should I then also say I am carless or bikeless or whether I own a home or not?" she wrote. She would rather call herself a free woman or a woman, period. Visualizing her future, a year or two ago, she had this image of standing powerfully in the world, with a man at her side and within a community, both of them supporting her to live her mission. "I clearly felt that children would be an energy drain. This vision released me from the conditioning that makes it seem so natural to want children. Since that time, I fully enjoy my freedom. I do, funnily enough, feel clear mother energy flowing through me, which doesn't necessarily have to be applied to children. My sense is that in previous lifetimes I have done my share of birthing and raising children. Great that I don't need to do that this time around."

I posted a reply as well, stating that I felt not an ounce of regret now that I am in my sixties. I also confided to never having had the wave of hormones I had seen prompting friends of mine to throw the pill into the bin and caution into the wind in a blind urge that a child had to be made as soon as possible. In my interviews, several other women mentioned that they weren't sure that their resolve for childless living could have withstood such an onset of the mysterious molecules produced by our glands, which spin our thoughts and feelings on the biological urge to procreate.

> "I decided at 27 to get my tubes tied, as I looked into the future and it held no vision of children at all. I wrote recently to the gynaecologist who accepted my reasons and treated me with respect, while the nurses gave me a hard time. I've had a really good life and never regretted my decision. I broke up with my then partner (who supported the decision) and married a man with adult children who have made me feel very welcome. I am now a step-grandmother, great-grandmother, great-great-grandmother, but we don't live near them and aren't involved in their day-to-day lives. Still not comfortable with small kids, I love my creative life."

> —Woman, 70, artist, writer and teacher, Australia

In her 1996 book *Beyond Motherhood: Choosing a Life without Children*, Jeanne Safer, PhD, highlights the same themes, based on her hard-won insights as well as conversations with four dozen women aged 22 to 72 from all over the United States.

True to her profession, this psychoanalyst's motto is, "No carefully considered decision, responsive to your real feelings, born of honest self-examination, will be the wrong one."

During her own years of ambivalence and anxiety about this life-defining decision, she had applied her training in self-examination to herself. "Would motherhood suit you?" is the basic question she advises women start to ask themselves early on. "Talk to your husband," she writes, "talk to your friends, and most important, talk to yourself—and listen carefully, with an open mind, to what you say."

For her own story, she dives straight in.

"Nobody will ever send me a Mother's Day card. No child of mine will ever smile at me, or graduate, or marry, or dedicate a book to me. I will leave no heir when I die." Realizing that motherhood was not for her was the hardest decision of her life, she writes, and the loneliest. "What would society think of me? What would I think of myself? What would the shape and meaning of my life be without a family? And what would I leave behind as my legacy?"

The journalist Alveena Jadoon recently wrote on the website Mangobaaz about Pakistani women who don't want children and their reasons. "In our society," she writes, "deciding not to have children is often problematic, because women here, as soon as they get married, are pressurized into having children. The option of not wanting children is never actually entertained."

The reasons given by the Pakistani women she talks to are no different from those given by people all over the globe. "I just don't feel like being a mother; I feel that I did not have to prove that I am a caring human being by being a mother; we are enjoying ourselves, just the two of us; I have witnessed other people having babies, and I don't want to go through it; I am afraid of childbirth; the world is a dangerous place."

Her plea on this online platform, which aims to amplify the voice of an alternative Pakistan, is for everyone to be more understanding and accommodating of the choices that people make, especially when it's something as personal as having or not having children.

Although these reasons sound credible, and we might get away with them, when someone asks, I wonder if they tell the whole truth. When we love someone, we might list all their marvellous qualities. Yet, adding them up will not amount to a full explanation of why we put up with their snoring or them leaving their socks on the bathroom floor and love them anyway.

There is this *je ne sais quoi*, this unpinpointable essence, which we will not be able to name, even if our vocabulary would have the width and breadth of William Shakespeare's 30,000 words. Eastern spiritual teachers say we cannot name the divine, seeing that every word we might find would be too defining, too small, too tight. We may only point at the underlying unity of all manifestation and beware of not then going on to worship the finger that does the pointing.

I feel the same goes for having children or not having children. Parents may name their love, the hormonal urge, their curiosity, but will that ever fully explain their wish to have children and their willingness to keep caring for them, even if they are a pain in the you-know-where? Likewise, we might list reasons for not having them, and these may sound plausible, but at the end of the day, what we say might point at the truth but not be it. I come back to our inner film reel. Only inwardly, in a place beyond words, can we know if children are for us or not.

I found a refreshing article on the impertinent question so often put to us—the 15 percent of women in the Western world who have no children—why we didn't, and the patronizing comment that we still will one day, on the website Sheknows, which calls itself a platform designed to empower all women to discover, share, and create. With its mostly upbeat articles it looks like a regular online women's magazine to me. In the Parenting section, however, I find a candid article by Christina Ferwerda: "Women Don't Need a Reason Not to Have Kids."

This freelance exhibit developer and writer thinks it is about time that women without children are asked about what we *have* chosen to pursue rather than being confronted for foregoing a lifestyle that doesn't fit us. She didn't have a particular "reason" not to have children, but, she sighs, stating that parenthood just isn't for her, is never the end of a conversation. She knows that she could get out of the trap by saying she is still looking for the right partner or that she doesn't want to burden the environment, but these weren't her reasons.

She recommends we turn the tables and ask, "Why are you asking about someone's reproductive choices?" This might make for a more interesting exchange of views than us trying to wiggle out of a conversation we've had so often before. Boring! Nearing the end of her procreative years, Christina Ferwerda is delighted that people are finally leaving the topic be and start to ask about her business and her projects. Her suggestion in general is, "Do not ask someone about their reproductive choices. Period. Instead, see the person. Ask about the things they *have* done in life."

I have breakfast with a friend, a father of three, who cannot quite comprehend why I am devoting my time to the topic of not having children.

"Isn't it all reverse engineering?" he asks, applying the technical term for deconstructing objects to discover the design to the reasons we tend to give for not having started as family.

"Why would anyone need a reason to express love in their own way?" he says over our fashionable poached egg and avocado on toast.

Another refreshing approach. Although I certainly am prone to think I have to explain myself whenever I say, "Thanks, but no thanks", he nails it. Just like parents, those of us who practise childless living don't need to come up with reasons why.

Unless we have clear reasons, of course, and we like to share, even at the peril of becoming evangelists for our cause. Unless, too, someone is truly interested, and we can have an honest and mutually enriching conversation. No need at all to pass that up.

13

Key Qualities: Unconventional and Autonomous

I n this spring part of our lives, we may not have had children yet or we may know in our bones that we will not have them at all. Throughout my interviews and research, I have wondered if there are traits shared by those of us who feel complete without children.

The first two traits that jump out at me are that we are unconventional and autonomous.

We are unconventional in the sense that we will not make the choices our parents made. Even if our numbers grow, we are still a minority, and that makes us stand out. We will need to practise a kind answer to the mindlessly asked question, "How many kids do you have?" by people who are trying to make conversation. They pick an angle that usually works well. We will need to find new friends when our old ones' conversations revolve predominantly around the plights of parenthood.

We are autonomous in that we don't let the expectations of others determine the course of our lives. More than a handful of us will have to fight for the right to make our own decisions—decisions that will steer our lives away from what might be expected from us.

In summarizing the spring of our lives—the years of growing up and getting to know who we are in the first place, the time of ploughing the ground and sowing the seeds for our future—here are two vital qualities that we may already be aware of or could hone to find blessings and bliss in our life without kids of our own.

Some of us are born unconventional and recognized by our family as such early on. Some of us are much more unconventional than we ever thought and need long years to adapt to who we turn out to be.

A Scottish woman I know wanted to live the life of a traditional 1950s housewife. Sure, she wanted to work first but then she wanted to meet the man and do the love-and-marriage-and-baby-carriage thing. She had it all planned out, from when she was a child through her teens and her twenties. She began to get a little worried when she hit her thirties, and now that she is nearing 40, she cannot help but conclude that the cherished image of how her life should be is a far cry from how her life actually has turned out. She loves her work, her home close to nature, her community. Yet, she can't quite get over being so much more unconventional than she thought she was.

From time to time, pictures go around on social media of blackbirds sitting happily on a line with a single white one between them or fish swimming in the same direction with one dropping out of the school and going the other way, going its own way.

Whether we were born unconventional or have needed to accept that we differ from the norm; whether we are accepted, subjugated, or rejected in our different way—the first thing is to accept ourselves completely, even celebrate our unconventionality.

As three of my nieces, all sisters, say, "Why dress like everyone else when we could look extraordinary?" True to their word what they wear is sometimes not beautiful to the conventional eye, but always interesting.

Extraordinary is actually a lovely word that comes from Latin. In that ancient language, *extra* means "outside of" and *ordo* is the word for "row, status, and order". The Romans already put these two words together over two millennia ago to describe what was beyond the rule, the habit, or the norm.

To this day, extraordinary has a positive connotation, and we might do well to adorn ourselves with this mantle. Let's celebrate our unconventional way of life, our swimming against the stream, even if we are the only fish in the pond to do so. Yes, at times it is painful and hard not to belong to the mainstream, not to be able to participate in these conversations on childrearing, not to be like the others. Who amongst us has never lamented that life would surely be easier if only we were normal, whatever we assume that to be? Yet, I bet we all know the feeling of self-empowerment, too, of accepting ourselves fully in all of our unusual, kooky, oddball selfness. Honouring our unconventional selves is a gift we can give ourselves any time of day.

Millennials these days cry out for the right to remain true to their innermost conviction that it would be wrong for them to bring a child into this world when parenting is not how they want to spend their time. They wish to get their tubes cut, tied, or sealed at a young age in order to remain in charge of their body and be able to have sex without needing to worry about accidentally conceiving.

Parents, doctors, and elders shake their heads. With experience to back them up, they wonder if this youthful verve will hold against hormones playing up at some unforeseen future date. But many millennials are adamant. They speak up for the autonomy to decide on this most defining of life choices. They demand the freedom to govern their lives as they see fit. Like every generation before them, they confront the previous ones with a new set of values, which are self-evident to them and somewhat unfamiliar to those born earlier.

Inexorably, however, we have been moving towards this point in history/herstory/ourstory, when women and men want to be in control of the way our life unfolds. We want the autonomy to decide whether we go into a relationship or not, and with whom. We want the freedom to go out and develop our innate capacities in meaningful ways through work. We want to be independent and have the power to make our own decisions.

Those of us who have remained childfree out of choice have paved the way for the next generation to see this way of life as a natural option when they contemplate their future.

Those of us who have remained childless against our will and made good lives for ourselves have in our own way helped change the sad image of the lonely woman or man into one of a highly functioning, happily autonomous person. We travel, we work, we lead independent lives, we develop ourselves, and we find uses for our talents in the myriad ways love has of expressing itself. Sure, we have our spells of loneliness, despair, and grief just as everyone does; yet, walking our own path is the biggest gift we could ever have given ourselves.

If we can feel that we are beings of light standing in our power, then life starts to make sense. It is a daily practice, one that brings a quiet feeling of joy, to foster that sense of autonomy, knowing deep down that all of us are a piece of the mosaic of life that we lay as one humanity, a mosaic in which every piece fits, no matter its shape or form. We are not done to; we do—our response to whatever happens in our lives is ours to determine. In that, we are fully and wholly autonomous.

Summer

Growth and Action

That time of year when the sun rises early and sets late, the fruits ripen, and fields are full of promise. That time of life when we make defining choices for a line of education, a field of work, a partner, too, maybe, and the ultimate choice of whether or not to have children. Paths start to diverge in this productive season of our lives that does not necessarily have to include reproduction.

14

Becoming Who We Are

The starting position is the same for all of us. We begin as children. In the process of going to school, getting an education, helping out at home, trying to find out what life is about with our friends, testing the boundaries of the previous generation, we are all travelling down the same street. We may journey at different speeds. The vehicle of the one may be rickety against another one's being shiny and fast. Some of us may shoulder responsibilities, when others are free to play. Yet, we are all kids growing up.

Until, that is, one of our friends takes an early exit to parenthood. The rest continue the trek down the main thoroughfare. When more and more people we know veer off to embark on children, however, our numbers dwindle. From being the mainstream, we suddenly look around to find ourselves on a road less travelled.

In a matter of a few decisive years, we who carry on as we were become the minority. While we linger with the papers over lazy coffee on Saturday mornings, members of the IPC (the International Parents' Club) scramble for groceries or scuttle their little league back and forth for parties, lessons, and sports. When we crawl into bed after a late night out on the town, they crawl out to feed the baby, pacify their toddler, or go to work at their second job. Many of them move to the suburbs, whilst we remain city dwellers or move somewhere out in the country without needing to mind if there is a good school in the area.

Our lives don't change much. Theirs are unrecognizably different from before they crossed the line from being a child to becoming a parent. Our timelines part, and those of us who are childfree or child-less generally need to find new friends with lives similar to ours.

15

Life Choices

At 18, my friend Em had a tough choice to make. From age three, she had been training as a ballerina. From age ten, she had been directing her own choreographies. With her long limbs and lithe body, she just loved to move and to dance. At the same time, she was top of her class at high school. University would be the way to go in order to satisfy her boundless curiosity. Yet if she went to university, she couldn't possibly also complete full-time ballet training, and if she opted to become a dancer, how would she satisfy her intellectual capacities?

Deep down, she had always known the answer: she was going to let go of the dream of being a dancer in favour of getting a degree and playing a more impactful role in the world. With her decision to pursue an MBA after finishing law school came a next choice, the one about children. If she was giving up dance, she wanted to create the optimal circumstances to work at top level. She knew herself well. If she had children, she would care for them so deeply she wouldn't be able to work day and night to make a difference. It was one or the other, a high-impact job or the deep intimacy of motherhood.

Again, the choice was as clear to her as it was painful. If she was to fulfil her destiny, babies were out of the question. So, in her early thirties, Em made the decision not to become a parent. When she met her life partner, she had already embarked on an international career. With a daughter from his first marriage he didn't see very often, he had realized that he wasn't born to be a family man. He'd much rather work late than rush home in time for dinner, so between them there was no issue about the choice not to have children together, and he thought the matter had been laid to rest.

That is why he was flabbergasted when, over dinner with friends a few years later, Em said that not a day went by without her re-evaluating their decision.

"What?" he cried, jumping up from his chair as if bitten by a snake. "I thought we had settled that years ago!"

"We have," she said in her characteristic quiet manner. Grabbing her husband's hand, she added, "and every day I verify if childless living is still the right choice for me."

Her husband threw his hands in the air and looked at their friends for support. He had thought that he knew his wife well. He had never noticed that she put their common choice to the test on a daily basis. For him, it worked fine to have taken a decision once and for all. He was delighted to have found a partner who didn't dispute his dedication to his work and didn't mind him coming home at all hours, as she did the same. He stomped around the table in anger and frustration that all these years she had secretly been contemplating reversing their common decision.

"I haven't been contemplating reversing our plans," she tried to explain. "It's just that I check in with myself about our choice every day. I revisit if I am still at peace with it. So far I am."

She has done what she set out to do: make the career, serve on boards of cultural initiatives, and be actively engaged in the lives of nephews, nieces, and countless other young and not so young people who seek her counsel. Like many others, she is the kind of person who conscientiously weighs her decisions, both personal and professional, considering and reconsidering what is right now.

> "A question I often receive after I tell people I am childfree is some iteration of, '... and your husband is okay with that?' I often reply with humour, by saying, 'No, not at all, so don't tell him, okay?' Then I follow with, 'Of course, he's okay with it! It was a topic of discussion on our first date!' What a weird question, but people do ask."

> —Woman, 39, assistant principal, United States

In some cases, the time to decide is short, and it is vital that a choice be made quickly and decisively as pertinent action needs to be taken with a morning-after pill or, in a later phase, abortion.

Many women have had abortions. Many more than I was aware of when I started the research for this book. We were too young, still a child ourselves, and our partner a mere boy or a fellow student or someone older who should have known better. We had a one-night stand. We had an affair. We used protection and still got pregnant. We had broken up in the meantime. We felt a child was going to wreck our future. We were just beginning our careers. We hadn't landed a secure job. We shared a flat. We weren't stable, emotionally, financially, or in the relationship. We were still recovering from our own childhood. We weren't in a position to provide for a baby or give it the love and care and chances in life any child is entitled to. We weren't meant to be with the father and didn't want to go it alone. We had other plans for our life. We might have wanted to want the baby, but we didn't.

We had lots and lots of reasons to verbalize what we knew in our gut must happen, or rather, must not happen. We made the decision from a place of pain, not because of malicious intent or because we didn't care. We would never knowingly want to hurt another living being, and yet we did.

Terminating the pregnancy broke us in a lot of ways, emotionally and spiritually. We put ourselves through the wringer and punished ourselves for what we did in harsher terms than anybody else could ever have. We didn't tell our parents. We didn't share with friends. Sometimes we didn't even let the man in question know. We have had to live with the choice we made, even if at the time we didn't feel we had a choice.

It may have been a long road putting ourselves back together, but we also picked ourselves up in the end. We live with the sadness. Though we have felt lonely beyond words and guilty towards the child and the family line that now comes to an end in us, we heal. Even if we still track the years ("She would have been 23 now"), we probably made the right decision. At least, that is what the women I spoke to told me.

"I see friends become parents, and their life is not attractive to me, which means I do not want to experience parentship in the way that they do."

—Man, 44, engineer, Kurdish

Ninety-five percent of women who have had abortions do not regret the decision to terminate their pregnancies says a three-year study carried out by UC San Francisco's School of Medicine's Division of Biostatistics. Between 2008 and 2010, the researchers tracked 667 women at 30 facilities across the United States. The sample group was diverse with regard to standard social metrics of race, education, and employment as well as pregnancy and abortion circumstances.

Sixty-two percent of the women already had children, which means 38 percent of them didn't. Of the women, 26 percent found the decision "very or somewhat easy", and 53 percent said the decision to abort was "difficult or very difficult". Financial considerations were the reason given by 40 percent of women; 36 percent had decided it was "not the right time". The overwhelming majority felt that abortion had been the right decision "both in the short term and over three years".

On the other side of the fence, anti-abortion campaigners cite findings from studies that say women who have had abortions suffer from feelings of guilt or regret as a result. The term "post-abortion syndrome", coined in 1981 by an American anti-abortion activist, has been helpful in claiming it as a recognized type of PTSD.

The 2008–2010 study makes a distinction between having lingering emotions after an abortion and regretting the abortion altogether. Post-abortion emotional reactions are normal, but they almost inevitably taper off over time, scientists say, and ultimately, very few women regret terminating their pregnancies.

Gloria Steinem, feminist extraordinaire, dedicated her 2015 memoir, *My Life on the Road,* to Dr John Sharpe of London. In 1957, a decade before physicians in England could legally perform an abortion for any reason other than a woman's health, he took the considerable risk of referring her for the procedure, as a 22-year-old American on her way to India. Knowing only that she had broken an engagement at home to seek an unknown fate, he asked her to promise him two things: not tell anyone his name and to do what she wanted to do with her life.

"Dear Dr Sharpe," Gloria Steinem writes, almost six decades of passionate activism later. "I believe you, who knew the law was unjust, would not mind if I say this so long after your death: I've done the best I could with my life. This book is for you."

16

Other Things to Do

Have you ever heard of hairscapes? I know landscapes, of course, and seascapes. Thirty years ago, roaming the spacious rooms of the Musée d'Orsay in Paris my mother, my sister, and I found ourselves gravitating towards a painting of boats, fishermen, women, and children at the seafront. This wasn't just any sea. Unmistakably, this was the North Sea, the sea that defines our country, the Netherlands.

There we stood, in the resplendent former railway station built for the 1900 Exposition Universelle, an art museum since the 1980s, gazing at that painting, recognizing the light at Scheveningen Beach captured by the Dutch painter Mesdag in the late 1800s, but not altogether comfortable with one another.

That morning at breakfast, my four-years-younger sister and her husband had handed each of my parents a mug for their coffee. Unpacking them, they saw that the text on these cups told them they were going to be grandparents. As the four of them celebrated her first pregnancy, I witnessed the rite of passage happen right over our croissants. In the instant of making the happy news known, my sister had crossed the channel that divides parents and children.

To keep it in Parisian terms, I felt like I still stood on the Left Bank of the Seine, La Rive Gauche, the unruly part of the city, while my sister had suddenly crossed the bridge to the establishment on the Right Bank. *Gauche* also refers to people who are somewhat awkward, unsophisticated, crude. And that's exactly how I felt—in acute pain over being left out, left behind, left sitting there empty-handed.

My mother dabbed her eyes with the white linen hotel serviette. My father kept slapping my beaming brother-in-law on the back. When was the baby due? Where were they going to live? Would my sister continue to work? Questions tumbled over one another in their four-leaf clover, and it dawned on me that I was probably never going to share such an affirmative moment of future family continuity with our parents, because I had other things to do.

In her 2017 book *The Mother of All Questions,* author, historian, and activist Rebecca Solnit writes a beautiful sentence that captures this moment of realization for me. In the title essay, she expresses her surprise that, after her talk on Virginia Woolf, the conversation focuses on whether this brilliant and troubled author should have had children instead of on her work and her advocacy against conventional femininity. "Many people make babies, after all, and only one made *To the Lighthouse,*" she pointedly observes.

In her own books, too, Rebecca Solnit is familiar with this zooming in on why a woman didn't procreate rather than on what she did create. She experiences it all the time. She cites many reasons for not having children herself. She is very good at birth control. Though she loves children and adores aunthood, she also loves solitude. She set out to write books and to have great adventures. She might have had kids and been fine—as she is now. Anyway, the question should not be asked in the first place, seeing as it presumes that women ought to be mothers and that this is public business, which it most certainly is not.

Every sentence in this essay touches me, and I would cite the whole thing here, but you had better read it yourself. Just one more quote from the book, because I have found no better expression of what I felt that morning, over 30 years ago, in Paris.

"One of the reasons people lock onto motherhood as a key to female identity is the belief that children are the way to fulfil your capacity to love," Rebecca Solnit writes. "But there are so many things to love besides one's own offspring, so many things that need love, so much other work love has to do in the world."

There is so much other work love has to do in the world.

Big thanks to Rebecca Solnit for these 13 words, which in my view say it all. She in turn thanks her long-time friend Paz de la Calzada—who, by the way, has no children, either—for the reproduction of six of her hairscapes in her book, oversize charcoal drawings of human hair, disembodied strands interweaving into patterns reminiscent of plants and ropes.

> "I chose my partner after choosing not to have children. My work, my creative expression, was always my foremost desire. It's not that I never believed I could work full-time and have children. In fact, as a young woman, when I was in college, that's all I believed. Professionally, there was no at-home or part-time path I could conceive of. It really simply is that children were not a desire. I do not feel it in my gut. I feel other desires in my gut: art, writing, spiritual devotion. It's as simple as that."
>
> —Woman, 43, former attorney/spiritual teacher/business mentor, United States

My sister turned out to be one of those people who can do it all—have four children, successfully start and build her own company, serve on boards, keep fit, maintain her friendships, and be a mother and wife her husband and children adore.

I salute those who have the bandwidth to play all these roles, as well as those of us who know ourselves well enough that we aren't even willing to try. I salute those of us for whom the pull to work has always been the predominant one. I salute those of us who have given and are still giving birth to projects and art works, to programmes and companies, to plans and innovations, to another way of living than has been the norm so far, to choosing to be themselves. I salute those of us who have mothered others in all kinds of ways, those who teach, support, and raise other people's children. For some of us, our career, clients, and co-workers feel like our family. We enjoy the freedom we have created for ourselves.

There may be moments when we see friends experience a type of love we cannot quite comprehend, when they are proud of their children, worry about them, or just love them. In those instances, we may wish we had the experience of that dimension of love, and regret may creep in, but we also see how demanding their children are. There are so many other things to do in the world than having to commit to this huge lifelong responsibility. We may be devoted to a cause that we give all of our free time to. We may love to hike or bike or trek. We may love art and travel to see it near and far. We may love animals, even value their company over that of humans in some cases. We may be fully dedicated to our work and have scant time for anything else.

> "My mother would make a wonderful grandmother, and both my sister and I have decided to live a childfree life. I regret she does not have grandchildren, because I know she would love that. However, that is not enough reason for me to change my desire to live childfree."
>
> —Woman, 37, marketing, did not specify a country

Let's be honest. Children take time, and if we want to work full-time, something has got to give. I know a few men who have given up their jobs to care for the children. I observe grandparents who fill in for working parents. I have been with teary women who confess to the high emotional price they pay in following their inner drive to make a difference in this world. Leaving their children with others day after long day for their regular job, their own enterprise, or business trips, they miss that irreplaceable moment their young daughter first leaves the house wearing glasses or their son shines in the school play. Other women have looked at their job and looked at their babies and, in spite of theories they might have entertained about motherhood, concluded that the latter take precedence over the former. Even with parenting partnerships nowadays, in which both parents do their share, in general, women still bear the brunt of organizing the household and caring for the kids.

Some, like my sister, are stellar multi-taskers, but many women either leave their jobs, start to work part-time, or look for employment closer to home with less of a focus on promotion and a career path to take them further.

Studies show how mothers take a hit in their salaries. This phenomenon has a name: the child penalty. The arrival of children creates a gender gap in earnings of around 20 percent in the long run. The wage gap between mothers and men is not a temporary slip. After the children have left home, women still earn less than men who might well be fathers. The child penalty for men is close to zero, but men in their thirties have told me that they cannot imagine having time for children.

"After spending two hours with my brother and his children, I have to go and stare at a wall for a couple of hours to recuperate," a man in his mid-thirties from Austria told me. He cannot comprehend how his brother survives his two toddlers. He also misses the friendship the two of them used to enjoy and feels that, because he wants to make a true contribution to the world of technological innovation, there is just not enough time for him to have children as well.

17

When It Doesn't Happen

Agood friend of mine was looking forward to the day when he
could start to teach his four, five, or six children to hike and
name the wildflowers, to ski and enjoy the mountains, to sail
and know the winds. When it turned out that he and his first wife
could not conceive, this sailor set a new course for his life straight
away. He became a pioneer in his field, and in that capacity has posi-
tively affected the life of many thousands, if not millions of people.

Whereas some are able make the switch from a traditional future
to navigating a self-shaped path swiftly, others are still mourning
what never came to pass years later.

For her 2014 thesis, Lois Tonkin, who specializes in working with
grief issues, interviewed 26 women who remained childless for social
rather than biological reasons in her country, New Zealand. Across
the board, her study participants said they felt misunderstood,
judged, unacknowledged, ignored, and isolated by others around
them. Many of these circumstantially childless women in their late
thirties and early forties talked about feeling like a failure.

One woman who speaks up for the involuntarily childless in the
United Kingdom is Jody Day. "Life is long, but fertility is short," she
writes in her 2013 book *Living the Life Unexpected,* in which she out-
lines a Plan B for a meaningful future without children.

Having had a disruptive childhood herself, Jody Day wasn't completely sure that she wanted children. After she got married, however,

she began to think of a child as the product of their love. She gave up her job to help her husband's interior design business grow, as this was going to support them as a family.

"Looking back on it now," she writes, "I can't quite believe how little thought I gave to these decisions; it's like I was following a script, and yet, if you'd asked me at the time, I would have said that I was an independent thinker."

Conceiving didn't happen for her, just as it doesn't for many others around the globe.

A study done in 2015 by researchers from the Center for Reproductive Medicine in Cleveland and university hospitals in Ohio states that infertility affects an estimated 15 percent of couples globally, which translates to 48.5 million couples worldwide who will for some reason or another not conceive, however hard they try. The scientists worked from the assumption that 50 percent of all cases of infertility are due to female factors alone, 20–30 percent are due to male factors alone, and the remaining 20–30 percent are due to a combination of both. With their novel way of calculating the odds, they find that at least 30 million men worldwide are infertile, with the highest rates in Africa and Eastern Europe.

> "I didn't pull out all technological guns, but at age 42 I made a low-tech effort to have kids solo. I was ambivalent, though. Not about the children, but about being a single mom, so I backed off."
>
> —Woman, 47, trainer and community worker, United States

Infertility can also be the side effect of a disease or of its cure. A formidable Dutch woman I know had cervical cancer at a young age. In order to save her life, she had to let go of her uterus. She went into early menopause and has remained healthy to this day, but going for motherhood was no longer in the stars for her. Another Dutch woman, who has made doing business in Arab countries her business tells me how, in the course of pursuing IVF with her then-partner, she was diagnosed with breast cancer. From that day forward, she became a regular visitor of a different ward in the same hospital. When she was done, so were her chances of motherhood.

"The choice to not have children is much more complicated than a list of options," a retired American landscape architect wrote in my survey. "The sequence of life events, such as the death of an older sister from cancer and a following death of my mother in my twenties, led me to a decision that was tested and revised many times."

She is right, of course. Deaths in the family were the deterrent for her; for others, the restraints lie in an abusive childhood. Some of the comments posted revealed worlds of pain that either prevented them from having children of their own or had them resolve that they had better not become parents themselves.

"Our childlessness stems from my past," wrote a 38-year-old Dutch woman, who works as a planner in individual health care. "I was sexually abused as a child, so having physical contact is often not an option for me. With therapy, I have managed to come to terms with what has happened, and I have pressed charges after all these years. We are able to deal well with being childless, although at times I feel frustrated and sad that this is the consequence of what happened to me back then. The childhood abuse affects my whole life."

In interviews, too, women spoke of cruel mothers and absent fathers, or the other way around—overbearing and intrusive fathers and mothers who looked the other way. It took years of hard work to overcome the anguish, shame, and pain, and for some us, the childbearing years are over by the time we feel we are healthy and balanced enough to be able to give a child what it needs.

18

A New Narrative

When the long and longingly held vision of children doesn't pan out, we have to find a new narrative of what our life is about. Jody Day speaks of a deep pit of grief in her 2017 TEDx Talk, "The Lost Tribe of Childless Women." She lists the losses of the involuntarily childless, such as never taking that first-day-at-school photo, never being part of the community of mothers in a society that equates womanhood with motherhood, not becoming a grandparent, not having a natural heir to bequeath our treasured possessions to.

She is astonished, she says, that she survived the harrowing initiation into this tribe of 1 in 5 women who remain childless in the United Kingdom; 1 in 4 in Ireland, Italy, and Australia; and as much as 1 in 3 in Germany and Japan, who are hidden in plain sight. "Grief," she says, "is a language my tribe speaks fluently, while society is deaf to it."

A useful distinction is the one she makes between the active process of grieving and being in grief, which might surface at any time, even much later. She also acknowledges how the grief she experienced and thought she would never overcome has allowed her to grow, as she observes how grief transforms the devastation of loss into an unsentimental ability to face reality, to accept life on its terms, not on ours.

With her online membership platform Gateway Women, this outspoken advocate for women who remain childless against their will offers a safe place for mutual support and starting to assess how to move on and plan for a life of meaning.

After telling her story of painful years of trying, the American author Pamela Mahoney Tsigdinos dedicates the second part of her 2009 book *Silent Sorority* to how a woman can rebuild herself "as a non-mom in an era dominated by Mom's Clubs."

She bases her advice on the five stages of grief, sometimes called DABDA, as identified half a century ago by the Swiss-American psychiatrist Elisabeth Kübler-Ross: denial, anger, bargaining, depression, and acceptance.

"I'd read about infertility," she writes candidly, "but never heard anyone actually acknowledge dealing with it. Apparently infertility didn't discriminate. It affected men and women of all races, colors, and creeds equally. For eons, it had struck families here, there and everywhere—sisters and brothers, aunts and uncles, friends, colleagues, and people crowding malls or strolling through parks."

She describes how on one lonesome evening in the midst of what she calls "her identity crisis", she wrote a post on the Internet about the sense of failure she was feeling. It was the first time she had acknowledged publicly that she was infertile. Almost immediately a return comment came from a woman in Australia, who blogged on exactly what she was thinking, what she felt, what she was living with.

It might take longer for some than for others to invent a new story, come up with new mental pictures that reflect who we are rather than who we thought we would be. One man, when he found that he was the cause of him and his reluctant wife being unable to conceive, resolved to become a teacher. He considers the loss of income and status he incurred a small sacrifice compared with the joy he finds in being around teenagers all day. He has created what he wanted in his life—contact with young people who, as it turns out, don't necessarily have to be his own.

A single Dutch woman in her fifties has, after many IVF attempts with a gay friend, concluded that her life is like "a sabbatical that I had better enjoy". This tireless worker pours all her energy and expertise into her coaching school, thus creating a widening circle of conscious awareness.

A Swiss woman discloses that it took her years to realize that although the door to having children remained closed, many others were still open. Instead of leading the conventional life she had foreseen for herself from a young age, she has held jobs in various parts of her mountainous country, living separately from her husband with whom she has been together for over 30 years, keeping their relationship fresh.

"Life is full of opportunities," she mused on a quiet weekend afternoon, sitting by the sunny window of their city apartment with her husband out running errands. "You just need to step in. My husband and I made a vow that we would be there for the children of others. With no medical reason to prevent us from conceiving, but it not happening anyway, we stopped when in vitro or sperm injection, ICSI, were suggested. A soul must also wish to incarnate, and I was crystal clear in not wanting to force this destiny. What we did instead is enlarge the concept of what constitutes a family. It was a big moment. A shadow lifted that I hadn't known hung over me. I fell from my head into my heart."

A Lebanese woman shares her wisdom with me. She, too, had assumed she would marry and have a family. Instead, she works like mad, spending the free time she has from her nursing work on social projects. She declares herself very happy. "As with many other things that I might like otherwise, I say *'Litakon machiatouka'* or 'If this is God's will, I accept,' and immediately I feel grace and deep gratitude for my life."

She calls herself a practitioner, this woman, and her eyes shine when she touches into her faith. What she practises is at the base of all great wisdom traditions, overcoming personal preference in light of what is, surrendering our will to a greater will.

The shortest pertinent teaching I know comes from Buddhism: "No self, no problem." We can overcome hindrances to our natural state of happiness, followers of this spiritual path say, by acceptance of what is. When we don't want anything different in our circumstances, we will experience equanimity and even bliss that is not dependent on anything. A spiritual approach will not fix things for us on the outside, but it will help us adjust our beliefs and self-image.

Acceptance of the inevitable is a simple, but by no means easy, time-honoured way to be grateful for what we do have when our preference would have been something else.

19

My Summer

When most of my friends from university had found their life partner, started jobs with major firms in our country or abroad, got a mortgage, bought a house, and had their first babies, I found employment with one of our country's largest banks as editor of their monthly staff magazine. My friends frowned at my enthusiasm for this periodical that, long before the arrival of the Internet, I saw as the only way for staff to stay informed about where the bank was going and how they could keep themselves current. It is hard to believe now but only in the 1980s did management literature proclaim the importance of people within organizations.

I rode that wave, as I left the bank to start out as a freelancer and subsequently buy the communications company of my biggest client. Upon doing so, I found myself sharing an office floor with one of the three women from the article that had so appealed to me in my student days. Thank you, goddesses of fate who spin the yarn of our lives. Thank you, power of intention that makes the universe move so we may bring our true self to life. Thank me, too, who listened to my dream and stepped off the beaten path to forge my own.

To be honest, I was also quite forlorn at first, with my old friends residing in baby-land and new friends not yet in place enough to share my innermost feelings with. Having been a painfully shy child, I still did not find it particularly easy to connect with people and, of course, I worked around the clock. After a first lonely period, I found most of my new friends through work. Freelance colleagues, graphic designers, and single people who had also moved to Amsterdam became my new companions. And many of us have stayed close to this day.

I had no real relationship for years, until I met an Israeli man who travelled between three continents for his work. Seeing each other every three weeks for a long weekend or so, we led the ultimate yuppie (young urban professional) life of those days. It was a wonderful affair, and when it was over, it was over.

> "If I had been a heterosexual woman, I would have considered having children. In the mid-1990s when I came out as a lesbian in my mid-twenties, it was extremely unusual for gay/lesbian parents to have families (in my circle of friends anyway). Now it is much more common . . . If I had been surrounded by lesbian parents etc., at a younger age, who knows, I might be a parent now? However, this is not something I regret. I am extremely happy and fulfilled in my life."
>
> —Woman, 48, film programmer/writer/PhD candidate,
> United Kingdom

Then, at a friends' house, I met an artist, Jos van Merendonk, who had been painting with the same colour green for over three years. I was impressed by his professional persistence, which he then applied to winning me. My sense of myself was that I could only hold my own with a man at some distance, but that was not what he had in mind. He had fallen in love and wanted to know and celebrate me, be there for me, and feel at home with me.

I almost choked from fear of being caged once again, my wings clipped like I had felt happen before. On one of our first dates, I postulated that I would never marry. He was unfazed. Just as he was unfazed by the fact that I was taking my temperature every morning to find out when I was ovulating, just in case I still, after all these years and with all my misgivings, would want to have a baby.

Almost forty, sharing my bed now with a man who had gotten a vasectomy when he was 35 on the grounds that he never wanted children, I continued to mark my temperature on the chart. With my temperatures lower every day, I had drawn extra lines at the bottom.

One day, I handed Jos the thermometer as I couldn't make out what it said. As he was making the effort, I started to laugh. I realized this was not because of me being cold, but because the battery of the purposefully bought device was giving out.

That evening the two of us had a good cry together, as I realized that my desire for a child was not and had never been big enough to see it through. Even if, for the first time in our lives, both of us understood that love has its own way of pushing people into parenthood, it was not on our inner film reel.

20

The Selfish Question

Men tell me they don't get asked whether they feel it is rather selfish not to have children. Women tell me they get or have got this question all the time.

Before the American author Laura Scott began researching her 2009 book *Two is Enough*, she knew very little about the motives and rationales behind people's choices to remain childless. She knew her own: being content as a childless person; valuing her time, freedom, and independence to pursue her passions; and loving her childfree marriage and their peaceful and quiet household. These were her paramount reasons for opting out of parenthood. She was interested in what compelled others to remain childfree, and how they got to this decision. Seeking out people who believed they could have had children but made the choice not to, led her to understand that making the choice is often just one stage in the process.

Laura Scott signals that as regards the decision-making process, the couples who chose not to have children operated from a different mindset than usual. First, they did not have the expectation that parenting would be a rewarding experience. Even if they had friends who delighted in parenthood, the couples Laura Scott talked to retained a measure of scepticism. Secondly, they didn't necessarily regard parenthood as a critical stage in their development or a sign of their maturity. They imagined another path by which they would grow and evolve as human beings. Some admitted that they thought they would be terrible parents. Others felt that, after some deep soul-searching, the only way to be true to themselves was not to have children.

The issue at hand is, Is this selfish?

It is in the eyes of some, maybe of many. It certainly is in the eyes of Pope Francis, who is noted for his interest in the poor, his commitment to interfaith dialogue, and his interest in climate change. Off and on since he assumed office in 2013, however, he has pointed his arrows at couples who choose not to have children, declaring this decision a selfish act.

"A society with a greedy generation, that doesn't want to surround itself with children, that considers them above all worrisome, a weight, a risk, is a depressed society," he recently said in one of his outdoor addresses at St Peter's Square in Rome, the capital of Italy, which has recorded a steady decline in its birth rate. "The choice not to have children is selfish. Life rejuvenates and acquires energy when it multiplies: it is enriched, not impoverished."

It will escape no one's attention how strange the allusion to selfishness is from a man who has chosen a celibate life in order to devote himself fully to his religion. Born in Argentina, he worked briefly as a chemical technician and nightclub bouncer before he was ordained a Catholic priest, so he knows something of the world outside of the Church.

What does he know of our motives? Well, he has his suspicions. He has spoken of a "culture of well-being" that can come when a couple does not have children and has the money and freedom to take nice holidays and buy a second home in the countryside.

"It might be more comfortable," he said, "to have a dog, two cats, and the love goes to the two cats and the dog. Then, in the end, this marriage comes to old age in solitude, with the bitterness of loneliness."

> "People should be more aware about having children. Children shouldn't just happen. This irresponsible behaviour is an issue for other people, society, and the planet."
>
> —Woman, 33, freelancer, Italy

Some of us, dear Pope, may be hedonistic DINKs, as self-serving as some parents are, whereas others choose childlessness or remaining childfree for reasons that are not selfish at all. Women and men give up parenthood because they are carrying a genetic affliction that they do not wish to pass on to their offspring. Others do not wish to transfer traits from our parents from which we suffered in our childhood. We hold a fear that we might leave our own children as neglected, abused, or abandoned as we ourselves have been. On the other end of the spectrum, some of us are recuperating from overbearing parents who charted the course of our lives without noticing who we were. The threat we pose to the environment plays a role for a growing number of conscientious people, who try to limit their consumption and, therefore, decide to abstain from having children.

Realizing that the climate impact of having one less child in America is almost 20 times greater than that of adopting eco-friendly practices for an entire lifetime, Lisa Hymas, then senior editor of the independent online newsroom Grist, a few years ago proclaimed herself "a GINK: green inclinations, no kids".

Does one little child truly make a difference? A study published in *Environmental Research Letters* says the impact of one less child equals a 58.6 tonnes CO_2 reduction for each year of the parent's life. Compare this with, for example, going carfree, which saves emissions by 2.4 metric tonnes; avoiding airplane travel, which accounts for 1.6 tonnes per transatlantic roundtrip; or being a lifelong vegetarian, which saves 0.82 tonnes, then not bringing a child into this world certainly makes sense.

In their 2017 study, "The Climate Mitigation Gap", Seth Wynes of the University of British Columbia in Canada and Kimberly A. Nicholas of Lund University in Sweden looked at why educational and government recommendations miss the most effective actions individuals can take to address their carbon footprint. They found that having one less child is the first of four widely applicable high-impact actions that could and should be officially encouraged in order to reduce our individual carbon footprint on an annual basis.

Others amongst us have a spiritual calling and choose a life without children to devote ourselves fully to deepening our understanding of the mystery of the divine. We want to be of service through teaching, writing, supporting others on their path and, in general, living in a mindful and generous way. Some of us have cared for younger siblings because our parents were unable to, unloving, or even harmful. We feel we have done enough caring for a lifetime.

A growing number of us simply no longer believe in the one-size-fits-all recipe for a fulfilled life. We may be straight or gay, we might not identify with a gender at all, be bi-sexual, transsexual, asexual—whatever our orientation, we have looked at the menu and lost our appetite, if we ever had it. We may have other creations to bring into the world than those of our flesh and blood. We have braved our fear of being regarded as strange, left behind, having missed out, having regrets when it is too late, and of being lonely later in life. For many of us, dear Father, not having children is not so much a decision or a choice but a pure expression of who we apparently are.

I notice my irritation at the Good Shepherd's sweeping generalization that people who don't have children are more selfish than the rest of the population. That's why I love it that columnist Meghan Daum has used this oft-used criticism as the title of her 2015 anthology *Selfish, Shallow, and Self-Absorbed,* in which 16 writers expand on their decision not to have kids.

With this compilation, Meghan Daum has wanted to show that there are just as many ways of being a nonparent as there are of being a parent. "Some do it lazily and self-serving," she writes in her foreword. "Others do it generously and imaginatively. You can be cool about it, or you can be a jerk about it."

Not every childless author she approached was keen to contribute. Some replied that they didn't have much to say on the subject; others were afraid of hurting members of their family. The 16 essays she did gather run the gamut of feelings known to humankind. From being fiercely unapologetic and critical of society's sentimental imagery of motherhood to vivid descriptions of babylust, fear of future regret, and being besotted aunts.

Being writers, they bring fantastic sentences to the table, such as Laura Kipnis's "In retrospect, not having children feels to me like having dodged a bullet." Or Danielle Henderson's "If the biological clock were an actual organ, mine would be as useless as an appendix.”

Writer, actor, director, and producer Henriette Mantel collected another 36 women authors for her 2013 anthology *No Kidding: Women Writers on Bypassing Parenthood*. They, too, come with gem sentences, such as Janette Barber’s “Not having children is my biggest regret, and if I had it all to do over again, I would do exactly the same thing,” or Margaret Cho’s “My child would have my heart completely—having never truly given that over, in all my relationships in my life, starting with myself, I wouldn’t even know where to begin.”

These authors, who reflect so candidly on their choices and decisions and what life chose and decided for them, are no more selfish in my opinion than anyone else who tries their best at this unpredictable thing called life.

A Dutch banker turned self-employed consultant also defies the Pope’s suggestion that not having children is selfish.

“I care so deeply for my parents and my siblings, for my beloved and for everyone I know, and even for everyone I don’t know, that having a child of my own would make me feel too vulnerable. I would worry so much about the well-being of someone who was fully dependent on me that I don’t think I would be able to function at all, let alone as a parent.”

He and his wife met at a young age and knew straight away that they would spend their lives together. They talk about everything under the sun. They have, however, never addressed the issue of whether they were going to be parents or not.

“We didn’t need to talk about that. I knew I wasn’t cut out to be a father,” he says, “and my beloved was engaged in turning the acronym FEAR from ‘Fear Everything and Run’ into ‘Face Everything and Rise’.” He says it lovingly, glancing over at her in their former farmhouse, where his traditional wooden shoes stand at the back door. “My only regret is that I would have loved for the world to have a reproduction of her.”

An American hardware and software consultant is happy to offer his own take on the selfish question. This man, who sees it as his purpose in life to facilitate healthy evolution in people, organizations, and technology, makes the point that we need to embrace our selfishness.

"I fully own the voice in myself which is selfish. There are, of course, other voices which are sacrificial. That is the nature of how we evolve. The selfish voice in me values my freedom to be responsible only for me and not for others. I do believe we all need to embrace the voice in us which is selfish; to disown that aspect of ourselves is to have it go into shadow, where it can leak out and create unhealthy projections onto others. It is this dance of 'me' and 'we' which makes us human, and each voice needs to be honored."

Author and publisher Karen Rinaldi sheds yet another light on the selfish allegation, as she ponders her mother's remark about her upcoming seaside vacation with her husband and two sons: "I'll bet you can't wait to get back to work. Motherhood—it's the hardest job in the world. All sacrifice!"

Whereas this was meant to be sympathetic to her life as a working mother, Karen Rinaldi is stupefied. She argues that if we cling to the idea of motherhood as sacrifice, what we really sacrifice is our sense of self, as if it is the price we pay for having children. Motherhood is a privilege that many of us choose selfishly, she states. Procreating ensures that our genes survive into the next generation, which could be called selfishness as a biological imperative.

On a personal level, she goes on to say, bringing a being into the world that comes from us cannot be described as selfless. Selflessness in her eyes implies having no skin in the affair, whilst a mother is all in. Reframing motherhood as a privilege, Karen Rinaldi changes the whole game. She redirects the agency back to the mother, empowering her, celebrating her autonomy instead of her sacrifice. Raising children is hard work, but the same goes for every other meaningful activity. She sees motherhood as a beautiful, messy privilege and tending to children as the most loving yet selfish thing we do. Tell that to the Pope, so he lets the childless and the childfree off the hook.

21

Enough unto Ourselves

You might argue that writers such as those who contributed to the two anthologies mentioned in the last chapter do not represent the population as such, since like other artists and thinkers, they tend to be free spirits who crave silence and solitude in order to be able to create. They need to be good at being alone for long stretches of time whilst they sit and think or paint or write or mould. Some may prefer the buzz of a café or a co-working space, but a good many of us will have our own quiet corner or studio to ply our trade.

It is, however, a common trait in those of us who chose to be child-free that we like being by ourselves. Whereas we might be sociable, we also enjoy our own company immensely. We love puttering around the house, reading the papers for hours on end, going to a flea market without others in tow who may get bored before we have had our fill. We aren't shy about having a solo coffee on a café terrace or getting into a conversation with the neighbouring table. We don't mind being seen having lunch all by our lonesome—dinner, too.

If we have felt discomfort at entering a bar or a restaurant by ourselves, we find or have found ways to overcome this. We used to bring a newspaper or a book to read to give us the air of being engaged in a worthwhile activity. Nowadays, of course, we have our mobile phone, and no one looks twice at someone, neck bent at that particular angle, engrossed in their device.

We love to work at all hours, exercise when we please, keep our favourite foods in the fridge knowing they will not be eaten by a herd of hungry teenagers needing to feed their growing bodies. We enjoy the silence of our home or playing our kind of music at a volume that doesn't disturb anyone else. We make love on a Sunday afternoon with no threat of anyone entering our bedroom. We might not get dressed for the evening, but have a bath instead.

Does all of this outweigh the intimacy of children? It does for people like me and others who need a lot of time on their own—down time, nothing time, musing time, reading time, ponder time, home time, integration time, staring at the clouds time, nothing to worry about time, admin time, having a late-night stroll time, pruning time, lounging time, sleeping time, loving time, being with no one but ourselves time.

A Dutch woman I met at Pilates class told me that she and her husband of ten years leave each other be and love living together. Driving to France for their holidays, they have a great time in the car, she said, being silent for hours, zooming along, each in their own bubble of thoughts. She feels that their mutual ability to be by themselves allows her to be completely herself.

A South African friend in her early forties goes out into the wilderness by herself for hours on end, as does an Australian colleague of hers. They are both busy people, these two, but when they can, they carve out time to restore their energy through being by themselves in the woods and the hills, putting one foot in front of the other, listening to birdsong, enjoying the beauty of the landscape, the flowers, the wind in the trees and on their skin.

Apropos of my survey, a teacher from the United States wrote that even if she has worries and concerns about not having children, she also strongly agrees with needing her own time and space and having her own freedom. When she found herself unable to get pregnant, she didn't do anything about it. This chosen non-action left her feeling alone and isolated as she assumed that most people would immediately start to try and have kids in another way, whilst she and her partner upon getting the news, took other paths altogether, starting a business and going to grad school. For the first half of her thirties she beat herself up with thoughts like, "What woman doesn't pursue fertility and do everything possible to get pregnant? What type of cold-hearted and selfish b**** must I be to accept the news of infertility and happily move on with my life?" It was the guilt of this choice that ate away at her, not the infertility itself. She is just now starting to see that her worth isn't defined by the choice not to pursue fertility treatments.

Parents may protest that children give life meaning. They may look down their noses a bit as they justify their own existence, ranking it above our free and unbound way of living, no matter how we got there.

They do have a point, I dare say, although it may not be the one they are driving at. I see it as a huge achievement that we alone are responsible for finding meaning, fulfilment, and happiness in life. It is true that we will not see the world anew through the wondering eyes of our toddlers. It is true that we will not be applauding the loudest for our prodigy at a school play or be surprised by a keen young interest in trees, bees, football, fashion, or the solar system. It is true that we cannot cradle teenagers on our lap when their hearts are broken or share our wisdom when they come to us with questions about the meaning of life.

But it is also true that those of us without children of our own must find the source of joy and happiness in our own being. I distinctly remember advising my mother to find her own purpose and not seek fulfilment through what I felt to be a noose around my neck. She was merely taking an interest, she argued, but I felt she lived vicariously through me, and I resisted by becoming reticent and taking yet another step towards noncompliance on the parenting scale. I've heard this protest from others, too. How can parents seek meaning in their children, who then turn around and become parents seeking meaning in their kids? Why not just have a meaningful life in the first place?

Some of us do this by being highly sociable and active. Some of us find fulfilment in our job, our vocation, or creative exploits. Some of us concentrate on our own being and inner growth. In long hours by ourselves or alone together, we find meaning inwardly rather than as a result of someone else's exploits or existence. As I am convinced good parents also do.

22

The Single Life

I n her 2011 cover story "All the Single Ladies" for *The Atlantic* magazine, Kate Bolick wondered, "How does a woman move through
the world alone?" At age 39, she looked back on her mother's ideas
that she ought to be independent and emotionally fulfilled in a relationship with a man who was in every way her equal. Not for a minute did she and her youthful friends ever doubt that such a man
would be available at exactly the right time and off they would sail
into the proverbial sunset.

How many of us have been brought up on such delightful and dangerous fairy tales. We would meet Mr or Mrs Right, and all would fall
into place. Life would be wonderful from now on. However, when we
looked again, times had changed; women had changed, and so had men.

With the arrival of feminism, equality of the sexes, the birth control pill, and female emancipation, the fairy stories whispering their
promises of a happy ever after if only we could find that one-and-only
partner became confusing. Everywhere we looked, people were getting divorces and the institution of marriage seemed weak on its feet.
Around the world, people were finding new forms for sexual life and
love relationships. As it turned out, women didn't necessarily need a
man to have a child. Gay people could have children, too, and not
wanting children became a viable option, as was staying single.

For centuries, daughters were either supposed to marry the boy
next door or, better yet, someone from a higher station in life. If we

remained single, it was assumed we would look after our parents in their old age. Women could also become a nun, if we were from a religion that maintained convents, or perhaps a governess or nanny, but that was about it. It was unheard of for a woman to live alone and not have children—what was a woman for? Men who didn't marry or procreate were also an anomaly, albeit of the more entertaining kind. They might be a mad scientist, an elegant bachelor, a bohemian, or a clergyman living with a housekeeper who might not only make his bed but warm it, too, with the relationship forever remaining undercover, whilst everyone knowing or at least suspecting what was going on.

> "I'm a complex mix of I'd love to have had children for the good bits and the relationships, but am happy as can be not to have the worries and concerns that go with being a parent."
>
> —Man, 53, company director, United Kingdom

In many places in this day and age, non-parents still receive a certain measure of condescension from parents, as do single people from those in a relationship and as do singles without children from all and sundry.

Historically in the United States, there have never been as many unmarried adults as there are right now, especially young adults living without partners. More than half of Americans no longer consider getting married or having a child to be a milestone of adulthood. The Canadian press was also abuzz of late with the news that, for the first time in the nation's history, more people were living in one-person households than in any other arrangement.

Psychologist Bella DePaulo, who has never had a serious relationship or lived with a romantic partner, has made single people, their happiness, and the stigma they face the object of her studies. In her 2017 TEDx Talk, she proposes that we change our perception of single people. She celebrates that those of us who are single, by choice or by circumstance, have more friends, keep in touch with family, pursue what matters most to us, experience personal growth, and contribute more to the life in our towns and cities.

She denounces the marriage myth—what she calls *matrimania*—built around the romantic notion that we will find this one person who will fully understand us and meet all our emotional needs and we will never be lonely again. She notes that with nearly half the population single, Americans spend more years of their adult lives not married than married. Not just Americans, I would add. Single people come in all guises, from those who happily prefer casual sex to the widowed mourning their losses, from those in between relationships to those who have tried commitment and found it not to their liking. Bella DePaulo describes herself as single at heart.

In her 2015 book *Spinster*, Kate Bolick uses the term as a badge of honour, a sobriquet. Sentences from her journals of her college years, such as "A long, perfect spinster wish of a Sunday, read all day, took two naps", reveal her pleasure in being alone. Whilst many have this, it is still deemed a weird quality to admit to.

In May 1898, Neith Boyce, one of the five women Kate Bolick calls her "awakeners", wrote her first column for *Vogue* magazine: "I was born a bachelor, but of course, several years elapsed before my predestination to this career became obvious. Up to that time, people acknowledged threatening indications by calling me queer, while elderly persons who wished to be disagreeable said I was independent. … It hurt them to think that the unblemished escutcheon of the family should be invaded by the pen rampant and shirt collar, saltier wise, argent, of the bachelor girl." This was the opening salvo of The Bachelor Girl, Boyce's recurring column in praise of the single life.

> "I have a long-distance relationship, and while I do consider this person a partner, I also still consider myself single. At this stage of the game, I think both of us value the independence we have created for ourselves."

—Woman, 46, writer and teacher, United States

On the other end of the spectrum are the involuntarily single. Some of the most interesting women and men I know have never met someone they wanted to be with long-term, or vice versa. They would like, or would have liked, to partner with someone but somehow have not managed to team up with the right person. Hopeful it still might transpire, a brave number of them periodically scan dating sites and go to awkward meetings with strangers who, lo and behold, sometimes turn out to be wonderful people they have a good time with for as long as it lasts. Some of them do find love, of course, and for a few, a child might still be in the stars.

A Korean woman tells me how hard it is in her country to find a partner, as work leaves little time to socialize. The same goes for Japan. Traditionally, having children in such collective cultures was regarded as a duty to society or family rather than a source of fulfilment in its own right, as it is seen to be in individualistic cultures, but this has been changing.

French sociologist Muriel Jolivet, who has lived in Tokyo since 1973, teaching at Sophia University, wrote her book *Japan: The Childless Society?* about the reasons behind the steady fall in Japanese birth rates over two decades ago.

After the Second World War, one of the ancient ways that vanished was the willingness of women to slave away and lead a life of self-denial, sacrifice, and selflessness in service to their husband and children as well as his family. Young women from the countryside started to leave, with no intention of coming back to marry any of the kind farmer boys they grew up with and live like their forebears. In the cities, the prevailing work ethic was not favourable to finding a partner in the period during which she wrote her book.

In spite of continued government policies to promote marriage and parenthood, the number of single women and men, as well as people, unmarried or married, who are not having sex, has not declined one bit. Women who aren't married by age 30 are still seen as losers by the older generations. Their parents will be asked what is wrong with them. Often, these young women themselves find marriage and relationships too complicated to negotiate and the men too awkward and passive.

Recent figures show that nearly a third of Japanese people are entering their thirties without any sexual experience. Of 5,000 single people surveyed in 2016 by Japan's National Institute of Population and Social Security, 42 percent of men and 44 percent of women had never had sex.

In 2017, comedian Ano Matsui, then 26, told the BBC: "Once I asked a girl out, but she said no. That traumatized me. There are a lot of men like me who find women scary. We are afraid of being rejected. So we spend time doing hobbies like animation."

Artist Megumi Igarashi, 45, said to the BBC: "Building a relationship is not easy. A boy has to start by asking a girl on a date. I think a lot of men just cannot be bothered. They can watch porn on the Internet and get sexual satisfaction that way."

A whole industry has sprung up that has men standing in line for hours to spend a mere few seconds with the object of their fantasy affections: a young girl dressed up in her cute costume of choice. They are not allowed to touch her as she gives them a dazzling smile, and before they know it they are requested to make place for the next person. Men of all ages forego other pleasures, save up, staying in their rooms, with pictures of their idols dotting the walls, until they have gathered enough for the next event. Sex is regarded by many not as a vital part of life but rather as a pastime that some engage in and some do not.

In 2015, a record 14 percent of Japanese women and 23 percent of Japanese men had never been married. A new trend is that women go through the ritual of marriage in a bridal gown complete with all the trappings but a partner. This "solo marriage" is a way for women to experience the ceremony of promising, with family and friends as witnesses, not to have and to hold another, for better for worse, for richer for poorer, in sickness and health but themselves.

This phenomenon is on the rise not just in Japan but also in Canada, England, and the United States. Dutch therapists and coaches, too, have started to give workshops and "sisterhood retreats" on how to prepare for such a day of commitment to self. A plan for a big day of self-celebration may be frowned upon by friends, when they hear of these solo wedding plans, but many will still want to be present when someone has the guts to make such vows to themselves.

"I did have children in other lifetimes, and chose to be a single in this one. Fun :-)"

—Woman, 50, communications expert, Germany

Married or single, with or without children, we live in a web of relationships, an ecology of kinship and friendship and love that have their ebb and flow. I imagine there is a curve of distribution for single people like the one for keen parents, determined non-parents, and the many in between.

The curve for singles would show people like Bella DePaulo, who have no interest in a committed relationship, on one extreme and those wanting a partner but not fulfilling that wish or at least not on a permanent basis on the other. In between sit those who find high to moderate satisfaction in living alone. As time moves us along, we may change our perception of our status and, with it, our stories.

An Australian writer responding to my survey captured the many aspects of her current single life:

"I feel my greatest desire in life is to be a mother, but I am single, about to turn 35, and just haven't met the right guy. I'm not too picky, but I do have high standards when it comes to moral living and lifestyle that I believe are completely appropriate. I'd rather be single and happy than in a relationship with the wrong person. I know my calling and purpose and get to live this out daily through my work. I am incredibly fulfilled and love my life. I often feel that others expect me to be miserable that I'm single. They treat me like I'm missing something or I'm incomplete. In the workplace, I can be expected to pick up the slack for others who have to tend to their children. Of course, I'm always happy to help, but I feel like my personal time isn't viewed as valuable as it's not spent with family. It's my time and I can do with it what I want! And in a religious (even in a modern, well-known, positive) environment, I can be treated by some as if my life hasn't started yet and I'm in a 'waiting' season. Nope. I'm living my best life, and I love it. Sure, I have hope for the future, and parenthood will be great when it happens, but life is also wonderful right now."

— Woman, writer, Australia

23

Finding New Friends

"**C**ome a bit earlier so you can still see the kids." A Dutch woman wonders how she can let her friend know, without causing offence, that she is eager to talk to her and seeing the kids is not on her priority list. She doesn't intend to be unkind, but she just is more interested in spending valuable time with the friend she knows from her schooldays than with her children.

As babies come, friendships shift. Young parents all of a sudden have lots to talk about with other young parents, even if they didn't know them very well before or even at all. They meet each other at Lamaze class, at the clinic, at the doors of day-care centres, kindergartens, schools, or bus stops, where they drop their children off before hurrying to work or to chores back home. They meet in the park and at playgrounds. They relocate to streets full of family homes, with their children making new friends naturally and thus providing easy access for their parents. They exchange intimate details on technicalities of feeding and washing and changing of diapers that none of us non-parents will ever need to master. They talk about school choices, how to discipline their unruly ones, the sense of overwhelm from being stretched between family and work. They plan their holidays together to child-friendly places. They save to be able to give their children an education. They worry about them staying out late and doing heaven knows what. They ponder when to allow their teenagers to sleep together under their roof.

Friendship can survive paths diverging, but not all friendships do. As we remain occupied with what we were interested in before and recent parents discover a whole new world of delights, demands, and duties, we may drift apart. Whilst we may have been one of the first to hold their little one in our arms (complete with a self-made or over-the-top present) and they may be named after us or we may be asked to be their godparents, we will never in a million years be as interested in all that raising a child requires as fellow parents.

We are lucky, if we have friends who are able to separate their parenthood from the rest of their being, who remain curious and open and interested in life beyond their busy bubble. Over time, it will become harder to keep the contact going with those who bury themselves in the intense occupation of rearing their breed. This may not always be a choice out of intention.

Parents are not exempt from experiencing loneliness. Exhausted by work and the daily commute, many have no or hardly any energy left at the end of the day. In these production years, the dual track of both a job and a family doesn't leave much free time to spend with friends or even by themselves. I am aware, too, of marriages breaking up when the children are still young, and how taxing that is on all involved, emotionally and practically. I am aware of children born with disabilities or prone to illnesses who need extra care, and the heartbreak of knowing the harshness of what is ahead for them.

> "I always thought I would have kids in my twenties. Met my now husband at age 29. He didn't want kids and had had a vasectomy before we met. I decided I would rather be in an amazing marriage than try to find another guy that I might not be able to have kids with. Fast forward to age 35 . . . I had a uterine fibroid and needed a hysterectomy. I take that as the universe telling me I'm not supposed to have kids. I still get jealous of my friends having babies, but I'm happy in my childfree life."
>
> —Woman, 38, retail, United States

All this can be enfolded in the existing friendship, in my experience, on the condition that the parents are able to generalize. When they talk philosophically about the adjustments they face on a daily basis in a way that compares to the decision-making we all need to do, the conversation can remain interesting. If they fall into the trap of telling endless stories about their particular children, those of us without kids will at some point get bored. Feeling there is no place for our adventures in this setting, we will naturally seek out people with whom we can share in a reciprocal way.

It is a law of nature that we gravitate towards people who resemble us. We will find new people to befriend who have no children, either by choice or circumstance. We may meet them through friends or through work, through sports or clubs. We will soon find that we have things in common, such as free time in the evenings and on the weekends; interests we can pursue unhindered by a sitter's time constraints; and having the money we earn available to spend on our own interests, hobbies, and projects.

We need friends and acquaintances. An American friend in her mid-fifties affirms that she loves weekend mornings just with her cat and that she sometimes feels really lonely. Having recently moved for work, she stumbled upon a group of single women of all ages who go to the beach, lectures, and movies together. If you're there, great; if you need to keep to yourself for a while, that is also fine.

A pattern I have noticed that could do with more research is that parents usually know other parents of roughly the same age and the youngsters their children hang out with. People without children, in my experience, tend to have friends in a wide age range, as we gather them along the way through a variety of channels. We cultivate our own relationship with children of friends on an equal footing. We also befriend colleagues of all ages with whom we share common interests. We connect with parents whose children have left home and who have time on their hands again. Thus, many of us end up with a varied circle of friends that span generations.

24

Aunting and Uncling

"Have you gotten hold of them yet?" My mother had been trying to get through to my sister-in-law and my brother all day, convinced that she would become a grandmother today, April 1, 1985.

With her husband frequently travelling and her job in my town, my sister often stayed with me overnight. For months, we had got together to embroider traditional symbols on the sampler we were going to offer this soon to arrive first new-born in our family—an anchor for steadiness, a tree for family, a heart for love and, of course, the alphabet.

Sitting head to head in silent concentration for hours, crossing our stitches, I had come to a deeper understanding of the imagery of the good fairy and her role of benediction for infants. Since the mobile phone had not entered our lives yet, after my mother's call the two of us rode our bikes to the clinic where we knew my sister-in-law would be giving birth.

The evening porter let us through, and there we found my sister-in-law, all red and sweaty. Terrified, I thought she was going to die, but she gasped to my brother, who looked concerned and forlorn, "Can't we do anything without your family?" Sheepishly, we said we just wanted to make sure she was alright. She joked that she was trying to keep the baby in, as she didn't want it born on April Fools' Day, and could we please leave her to it.

We went back to our fairy godmother work. We got a call two hours later. Stephanie had come into this world. On our bikes we jumped again, my parents came, too, and hers would fly in from Norway the next day. I marvelled at how I could partake in the miracle of this baby, the perfection, the shortcut to a place in my heart that I didn't know existed, the prerogative to be allowed to hold her and kiss her and know that I would know this astounding being for all of her life, until mine would expire.

> "My sister is rather late with starting a family, so her son has come late in life for me, too. I now see the impact. If my sister and her husband or my parents as new grand-parents are conscious of this or not, my role within the family has been brought down a few notches. A blind horse could see that my sister doesn't only adopt the role of proud mother but also feels more important within the family, which is something I had not at all foreseen."
>
> —Woman, 41, artist/designer/caterer, the Netherlands

On the day that her nephew was born, Melanie Notkin made a picture of the sky to remember what the world looked like the day her life changed forever. When she cradled him in her arms for the first time, she felt a devotion, love, and joy she had never known before. Soon, however, she realized that as much as her nephew changed with every day, every week, her own life actually didn't change that much. It also dawned on her that as a professional single woman she didn't have a clue about how to fulfil her responsibility as an aunt.

When she discovered that nearly 50 percent of the adult women in the United States are non-moms, she found her new vocation. She coined and registered the term PANK® (Professional Aunt No Kids) to describe not only herself, but the growing number of non-moms who share a special bond with a child in their life. She launched an online community for aunts only, proclaimed the fourth Sunday in July to be Auntie Day for perpetuity, and wrote the book Savvy Auntie.

In this 2011 "ultimate guide for cool aunts, great-aunts, godmothers, and all women who love kids", she concentrates on the early years, when non-moms can feel at a loss about how to cook fail-safe foods for kids or help plan a birthday party. Whilst I never got to that level of detail, even when I had my young nieces and nephews staying over, I love how seriously this aunt is taking our role.

Dr. Robert Milardo is emeritus professor of Family Relations at the University of Maine. He grew up in a typical Italian-American family, with his mother's six sisters and his father's three brothers and one sister all living in the area. He has fond memories of the extended family visiting often. He remembers how he would seek out one of his aunts to complain about his parents. She would listen, acknowledge his stance, convince him that they were kind people, and he would return home comforted. He fell over on the first day of riding his bike, and one of the uncles who had been watching carried him to the kitchen for first aid. In short, he had a passel of second mothers and fathers who were interested, encouraging, supportive, playful, and always there, he recalls in his 2010 book *The Forgotten Kin*.

A visiting research appointment at Victoria University in New Zealand provided him with the perfect opportunity to dive into a new field: the relationship between generations. Remembering his own uncles as role models, with some to emulate and others with life-styles to avoid, he started with a handful of questions to uncles and nephews. Were they important to one another? What did their relationship look like? Did uncles complement the work of parents, and how did nephews regard them? On his return to Maine, paying tribute to his warm, quirky, inquisitive aunts, he added aunts and nieces to the study.

He knows the figures, of course, that say that close family members are common perpetrators of sexual abuse. In his sample of 104 participants he has, however, found no evidence of this. What he did find, was a decidedly generative culture of what, as a variation on the word parenting, he has dubbed "aunting and uncling".

Being a social scientist, Robert Milardo uses the term "generativity" in the sense of "a concern for future generations that include mentors, meaning keepers or family historians, intergenerational buffers, and fellow travellers or friends". Mentors are the practical guides who model action, teach skills, provide guidance or support, and generally facilitate the advancement of others. Direct mentoring of nieces and nephews occurred in nearly all areas of personal and relational life, according to his findings. Moreover, this mentoring is not one-way traffic from the older generation down.

Aunts and uncles described their roles to him in a variety of ways, often seeing themselves as adjuncts to parents, as third parties with a more objective perspective, or as surrogate parents. Telling him their stories, several come to a deeper understanding of their families, siblings and parents, aunts and uncles—how aunts and uncles are important to parents, and how they, in turn, are influenced and later in life supported or even cared for by their nieces and nephews.

Half of the uncles he spoke to and slightly more of the aunts had no children of their own. He explains this overrepresentation through the availability of time and the significance of the opportunity for aunts and uncles to be with children and participate in their upbringing. Some of them were present at the birth of a child; many have them over in childhood and make sure this time together is fun. In fact, Robert Milardo found that fun is one of the features that help fuel the intergenerational friendship.

I am struck by his use of the word "friendship". Relative to my nephews and nieces, I had never thought of myself in that capacity, until my philosophical nephew Thor named our relationship as such. I sat back for a moment, both puzzled and touched that he would regard me, 35 years his senior, as such. "Come on, Lie," he said with his winning smile. "You've been cultivating my friendship from when I was three." A beautiful case in point of how the younger generation opens the eyes of the older one.

Over time, as they grew up, I have had to adjust my relationship to my nieces and nephews. In my eyes, being regarded as a friend is one of the highest honours a human can aspire to. I felt like having been knighted that afternoon in my nephew's student room in London. I walked on air for a week. I knew how precious the offspring of my siblings are to me, yet I found it surprisingly hard to be acknowledged for how precious I am to them as well. My heart knows this. My friends know it, too, as I tell them of the struggles and successes of my nieces and nephews. My head, however, is still finding the proper place for this aunty love, which should not be too much, too overbearing, nor too little.

> "Family life is full of dynamics, which become apparent when we are together, like in holiday times. When brothers and sisters bring their new families, and you are excluded. Wisely keep mum, as 'You don't know how it is, because you don't have children' can fly by at any given time. Then being the aunt nieces and nephews are curious about, as she lives the freedom they strive for in the process of getting loose from parents. Showing them being true to yourself in action. :-)"
>
> —Woman, 57, consultant/sculptor, the Netherlands

Others have broken ground for this role that is markedly different from parenting, yet little studied. Speaking about her childlessness on one of Oprah Winfrey's Super Soul Sundays, author Elizabeth Gilbert commented that in her experience not every woman is destined for motherhood. She distinguishes among three kinds of women: some women are born to be mothers, some are born to be aunties, and some should not be allowed to be within ten feet of a child. She argues that it is important that we figure out which one of those camps we belong in, because tragedy and sorrow results from ending up in the wrong category.

"I'm in the auntie camp," responds Oprah Winfrey, who has often stated that she sees herself as mother to the world's children.

"Me, too," Elizabeth Gilbert smiles. "I call it the Auntie Brigade."

Childless aunts affirm the pleasure we derive from this role. One corresponds in handwritten letters with her nine-year-old nephew who lives abroad. Another has contributed to the school fees of her sister's children and spurs them on, now that they are in college, to find a job to sustain themselves, as she has done. One pledged to be a co-parent, when one of her sisters birthed a disabled child. Fourteen years on, she is true to her word, having her prized nephew over two nights a week, come rain or shine. Another acted as a third parent when her nephew was born with an incurable disease. The three of them nursed him through his days of agony whilst taking turns to care for the two older children.

An academic became the guardian of a nephew born to a much

younger sister and at a later date adopted this seven-year-old. "I don't have a maternal bone in my body," this wise woman said, who lives with a woman who is already a grandmother to her own two children's children, "but we cannot always choose what love sends our way, and I love him beyond what I thought possible."

My niece Stephanie drops by, and we talk about how our relationship has changed over the years. She is silent for a while, as she is wont to do, then observes, "As an aunt you are like an extra parent who I can talk to but who doesn't tell me what to do. You see us as grown-ups, and we have had grown-up conversations as long as I can remember."

Once more, I feel as seen as anyone, fortunate to have this young woman and the other ten nephews and nieces in my life, bashful that I am so appreciated by them, and moved, moved beyond words.

25

A Better Answer

Papers and magazines regularly publish columns and articles about what to say when people ask why we're not having any children. The trick is not to get defensive, journalists conclude, by and large. For some of us, this is easier said than done. Especially in the years that the biological option is still open or when it seems like it's not too late for us to be swayed, people who are parents can be quite insistent.

The trio of questions asked seems not to have altered in the past 30 years. "Don't you think that's rather selfish?" is usually followed by "Don't you think you will regret it?" and finally, "Who will take care of you when you are old?" If these questions are asked out of genuine concern, that's one thing. On the whole, however—we might be oversensitive, I concede—the tone of questioning is critical.

This is especially painful if we are in the process of reconciling ourselves with remaining childless. Whether this was our own choice or not, such thinly veiled judgements can hit home. People can also be really insensitive. Remarks like "Not until I had a child did I know true love, you know" imply that we never will. "A child has made me mature in ways nothing else could have" suggests that we will never really grow up. Not everyone will probably intend to hurt us, as they are talking about themselves, but such careless remarks can make us feel relegated to an obscure place in the universe reserved for weird folk who don't understand what life is truly about.

A journalist who has heard of my research calls for an interview on what to reply when people tell us that we will change our mind. She is 33 years of age, and for as long as she can remember, she has been convinced that she will not have children. Clearly furious about the impertinence of people assuming to know what is good for her, she asks me what I say. I tell her my answer has changed over the years. When I was younger, I confess to having frequently been on a self-appointed crusade against the old-fashioned assumption that everyone ought to have children.

> "Someone once told me, 'Give me a good reason why you don't want to have children', and I answered, 'Give me a good reason why I should give YOU my reasons'. I decided not to have children in my early twenties. When I was in my twenties and early thirties, people used to say, 'You'll change your mind as you get older' or 'You'll regret it'. Now that I am in my late thirties, when people ask if I have any kids and I say no, they say, 'Keep it that way'. I don't know if this is because of the age or because people are starting to see things differently."
>
> —Woman, 38, auditor, Costa Rica

A woman in her mid-thirties from India asks the rhetorical question, "Why would I want to be with my own children for the rest of my life when I could contribute to the well-being of so many other young people in marginalized communities?"

What she gets asked in her culture is not if she doesn't have children but why she isn't married. "I never found a good enough reason to do so," she says, "so I ask people, 'Why marry?' in return."

Her life choice initially troubled her parents, who expressed their worries about her old age or falling ill.

"I used to shout them down with arguments," she says, "but with maturity I can see the reason behind their concern. They wanted me to have someone to come back to in difficult times. That I can understand, even if I don't feel the need for such companionship. They themselves took in my two grandfathers and an aunt who was terminally ill. She was married without children and in the end, she lived with us. They have all died now, so it is the three of us again, or rather two and a half, as I am frequently on the road for my work."

Maturity is the key word. This refers to us growing in the awareness that people who love us are genuinely concerned as we tread a path unknown to them, in the self-confidence that we don't need to defend our choices as well as in the acceptance that people are sometimes just trying to make conversation.

Let's be honest: we, the childfree and the childless, can in our pain or pride on occasion be rather rude to those who inadvertently bump into us deviants from the norm. Hordes of people don't like having their major choices challenged, and with our opting for another way of life, this is exactly what we do.

Also, many conversations between people who meet for the first time are held on auto-pilot. We ask each other how we got to the venue, what we do professionally, and, especially amongst women, how old our children are and how many we have. This seemingly innocent exchange of information is part of the cultural codes of meeting and greeting, the ritual of sounding each other out to scan if we wish to engage in further conversation or move on to someone we might have more in common with.

When we break the flow of this initial conversation by saying that we have no kids, thank you very much, we leave the other empty-handed. We can be more gracious. The aforementioned Swiss woman, who was highly surprised when her marriage didn't lead to children, and who worked it out with herself and her man, pleads for clemency with those who thoughtlessly ask. "I say that, no, I don't have any children of my own, and yes, I am close to children around us, so I keep the conversation open."

As most of us human beings like to talk about ourselves, another approach towards an interesting exchange may be to disclose with mirth that we have none and ask the other, "What made you have them? And what has parenthood brought you?"

> "I'm engaged to be married. A lot of things contributed to me deciding not to have children, and the question, 'Why don't you want to have children?' bothers me in that I can't possibly explain in a sentence or two. It's personal, and it's not personal. There are reasons, but then again there aren't 'reasons'. It's just knowing that it's not what you want."
>
> —Woman, 33, public servant, Australia

At times, we may resort to an answer that ends what can feel like a third-degree interrogation. Not in the mood to explain the complexity of our inner world or relationship circumstances to a temp, a taxi driver, or our bank manager, we may shut them up by looking pained and declaring we just couldn't have any. Some of us have imaginary husbands, children, and even grandchildren for the same purpose, especially in places where, as women, we are severely pitied and considered too spooky to trust when it turns out we have no offspring. Some of us who travel to those regions frequently have a whole story complete with names, ages, and occupations ready in reply to the inevitable questions about the home front.

The journey towards a gracious answer is well illustrated by an American woman, a lively 54-year-old redhead with freckles to match. Recently having relocated, she had to find a new answer for people she was meeting for the first time, who invariably said well-meaning things like, "Welcome. Nice to meet you. How many kids do you have?"

She readily admits to having long harboured feelings of being socially inadequate as she has never been married, is not in a relationship, and does not have children. "Ten years ago," she said, "these kind of questions would have reduced me to tears. Even though I came from a broken home, with a mother who disowned us when we were teenagers, I always pictured my future as one of marriage and motherhood."

She grieved long and hard when that vision didn't materialize, asking herself who she was if she wasn't a mother. "I came to the conclusion," she asserts now, "that without having given birth, I am still a nurturing and loving woman. I care about people."

It has taken a good amount of inner work to get to the point of not shaming others for their auto-pilot question, but she has found an elegant answer that lets both her and the one making the casual query off the hook, "None," she will say now to people she meets for the first time, "but I have a nephew and a niece whom I love and support," sometimes throwing in for good measure, "and a cat."

Giving credit where credit is due, some people are quite sensitive. They visibly gather their courage to broach the subject of whether or not we have children. They tread with care in their enquiry. Hence, giving them an answer is not only easier but we will be inclined to be more truthful, too. If we are willing to be open and honest, so will the other person, and many a good conversation can be had.

Another topic that may make for an interesting exchange of views is how people feel about us being granted a sabbatical in lieu of maternity or paternity leave. We could get this, men and women, once we have taken definitive measures to prevent us from conceiving or after age 40 for women, unless we have frozen our eggs. The details would have to be worked out, and conditions for parents differ across the continents. It would make sense, though, that those of us who do not parent should receive a period of free time equivalent to the average number of weeks that colleagues are granted maternity or paternity leave.

26

Key Qualities: Self-Starting, Self-Directed, Self-Sufficient

Roads diverge during these productive summer years of our lives. Friends and colleagues who become parents start to lead a different life, with a different timetable from those of us who continue as we were. Some of us spend long years, during this season, trying to conceive or to find a partner to start with. Many of us brave queries into reasons why we don't do as everyone does, whilst we courageously shape our future according to the truth as we know it in our hearts.

Reflecting on the conversations I had and the stories I heard, I see three interconnected qualities that make for joyful childless living in this active season of our life—self-starting, self-directed, and self-sufficient. We may always have possessed these traits and we may need to hone them.

That is a lot of "self" in there, one might object, especially for people in collective cultures in which the emphasis has always lain on conformity, interdependence, and embeddedness in a broad social context. Individualistic cultures tend to be more focused on autonomy, independence, and uniqueness.

At the University of Waterloo (in Canada, not Belgium), researchers have reviewed data collected between 1960 and 2011 from 78 nations around the world. The data formed part of the World Values Survey, investigating the importance that people place on friends versus family, how important it is to teach children to be independent, and the degree to which people prioritize self-expression as a national goal.

Over this half a century, according to psychology researcher Henri C. Santos and his colleagues, individualistic practices and values have increased across the globe. We are freeing ourselves from living pretty much the way our parents and grandparents did. When the age-old moulds no longer fit, we need to expand the playing field. That is what these three qualities help do.

At heart, being or becoming a self-starter involves taking the initiative. Without little feet running to our bedside in the morning to get us up and make breakfast, we need to find our own reasons to get up and get going—curiosity about what the day may bring; engagement with our work, our family, and our friends; a cause that motivates and inspires us. Whatever it is, coming into action is an inside job. Whilst work might provide a schedule for the day, it is up to us to muster the spunk to organize a dinner party for friends or people down the road with whom we want to get acquainted. We need to become enthusiastic and take the initiative if we are to follow through on getting tickets in time for that game or concert we know that we and our friends would enjoy attending together. If we want to take a hike we need to get up from the sofa, or get a dog trained to carry its leash to us when it's time to sniff out the neighbourhood.

Without a mini-me (or more than one) whose schedule determines ours, where we live and how we go about our work and social life is entirely up to us. Having said that, being self-starting is also like email, in the sense that the more emails we send, the more we receive. When we are socially active, in whatever way we choose, we become part of an active flow, in which we alternate in organizing get-togethers with others, and no one keeps tabs on who does what.

Seeing life as a permanent dynamic process of creation is at the core of being or becoming self-directed. Within parameters, such as having to earn our keep, we can pretty much fashion our life as it suits us best. We direct the movie, write the script, and play the lead.

Not having to live close to good schools (unless, of course, we are teachers), we may want to stay close to our family or, to the contrary, move away and find new fields to play in. We may love city life, the woods, the water, or the open plains. We are free to direct our gaze towards the place where we can flourish, without having to accommodate youngsters and their irrefutable needs.

Freedom is the benefit of life without children that most people rank first; freedom, however, isn't necessarily easy to negotiate. It can even be quite frightening to realize that nothing is a given and the content of our days is up to us to shape and form and give direction to.

Being self-directed requires that we monitor our inner compass, with its needle unfailingly pointing to what is ours to do. We may follow the direction it points in or pretend it isn't there. We may lend our ear to our rational mind, which will produce endless arguments about why we should or should not venture out and be different. Reasoning is what the mind does really well, but it cannot come to a decision, as it will always see the perks of the other side as well. Without denying that some decisions need weighing and reflection, our life in the end is not up to our mind to direct. Our heart will sit in that chair, and it will navigate its course according to our inner compass, which will point us in the right direction. Then it is up to us to trust ourselves enough to follow our own footsteps.

Can our own company be enough for us? Can we find gratification in our own being? Can we experience joy that comes not from another person's existence but just our own? This is the yardstick. This is what will make or break us in our childless and childfree lives. This is the quality we build and hone, stemming from the previous four. If we can embrace ourselves fully, be sufficient onto ourselves, we are made.

This doesn't mean that we will retreat from public life. Quite the contrary: we are social creatures like all other human beings. We need contact and appreciation, fun and games, laughter and shared grieving over inevitable losses as much as the next person. Being self-sufficient, however, means that we don't depend on the life of another running smoothly for our own happiness. Or, to put it more bluntly, we don't hang the weight of our fulfilment around the neck of another human being, often a child.

Not all parents, of course, but a good many live, as it were, through their children. If their child is happy, they are happy; if their child is going through a hard time, they don't feel so good. This is both the beauty of the parental bond and the price of it. We can either feel we miss out on what may look like an essential human connection, or we can rejoice in our self-sufficiency. There is true power in feeling that we derive none of our well-being through someone else's; that we are utterly complete in ourselves.

Autumn

Harvest and Reflection

This is the period of taking in the crops, of fruition and returns, of culling and yielding—leaves turning to gold in the lessening sunlight and temperatures dropping, but for days of unseasonable Indian summer warm breezes. The autumn of our life is when we begin to reap the fruits of the efforts we have put in and the experiences we have gathered. We know ourselves now. We've come to terms with who we quintessentially are. We are present with what is and poised for what life has in store for us in this second half of our time on this planet, and for those we love, children of others included.

27

Being Present

We each have an unmistakable presence. We all know how the atmosphere can change when someone enters the room. The mood alters, the conversation shifts.

At a recent reunion of my high school class, I was struck by how much I recognized the presence of each of the people I had shared those forming and storming years with. Whatever we had become in the way of work and relationships, we were still the same people. We had not changed; we had matured, like whisky grown richer in texture and taste through the years. It felt good to be in their presence again, all still healthy, none having to prove their worth any longer, each having had our blows and our blisses, more mellow now, more interested in the other than in ourselves.

In the autumn of our lives, we become aware of the unknowable but certainly more limited time of active participation we have ahead of us now. We may drop down dead tomorrow, have to deal with disease soon, or live well into our nineties.

Some of us wake up in the night with a start and remain awake worrying about who will take us to the doctor's, who will manage the business of our lives when we fade, or who will sit at our bedside when we die. Worrying will only cost us a good night's sleep and not solve our issue, we know, yet our fearful mind may torment us like a night porter opening doors of existential fears we have little defence against in the dark.

In the light of day our apprehension will lessen, but still, when we need to fill out a form and give a name for someone to contact in case of emergency, if we are single, who can we ask to be there for us in need? Our nephews and nieces might be too young or too busy with their own lives. Our potential emergency contact person may not be a close enough friend for us to feel that we can shove ourselves as a potential burden in their direction.

We talk with friends and agree that we will be there for one another. We name each other in our wills, but we might have a stubborn voice telling us times of hardship are to be shared with family. The sense of tribe and clan is stronger than we thought when we feel into these life-and-death matters. How do other people without children do this, we wonder, as we postpone addressing the topic. We'll look at this next weekend, or over the holidays, on that famous "rainy day".

> "Raising children is a significant life-long commitment and responsibility that in my perception would narrow my potential for contribution to something greater."
>
> — Man, 65, grower of plants and people, Canada

Some of our friends become grandparents. We register their joy, and some of us have to go through the misery of jealousy once more, feeling short-changed, missing out yet again on ineffable intimacy and pleasure now in seeing a child of our child discover the world anew.

Others amongst us, myself included, count our lucky stars that we are still free to roam, even embark on a second or third career, if we choose. We still have so much gusto, and in this autumn season, we grow into elders who have seen a lot of it before and can give wise counsel. We bring our presence, our not-honed-by-children-but-by-life views, and our eclectic, maybe eccentric experience.

In her 2014 gilt-edged hardcover book *What I Know For Sure*, Oprah Winfrey tells the story of how for once she was lost for words when film critic Gene Siskel asked her in 1998, "Tell me, what do you know for sure?" She falteringly replied that she was going to look into this and she did. The undisputed queen of opening people up through her presence has since explored this beaut of a question in every issue of her magazine, and the book is a compilation of those columns.

One recurring theme is that of having to face our mortality without flinching or turning away and to live in the space of thankfulness. We are still here; not everyone has made it this far. The choice to flounder or flourish, she points out, as she did for a quarter of a century in her daily show, is in our own hands. It is up to us, in the autumn of our lives, to find time just to be and to listen inwardly to what is ours still to do and be present to.

28

Wisdom Years

The question of what makes a mature adult has many answers. A woman might say, "Having gone through the miracle and agony of childbirth and survived."

People in war zones, places of drought and famine, or refugee camps might concur that knowing how to survive in extreme circumstances has made their children into premature adults, as exhaustion, danger and death loom on a daily basis and still they must find ways to continue.

In other circumstances, the answer might be, "stepping into the lineage of our ancestors. It is through their wisdom and cunning that we are here in the first place, so we must honour our past and uphold their ways."

A third viewpoint is, "Life is a jungle, and we each need to look out for our own, whatever it takes."

Adherence to the law is yet another reply, overcoming youthful rebellion and becoming responsible citizens who conscientiously go about our work, raise our family, vote, and pay our dues.

Another is, "Someone who is smart enough to create opportunities, forge strategic alliances, and scale up to reap the benefits and enjoy life to the max."

Those who have woken up to the plight of the planet might say, "Mature adults see themselves as part of a global community and are conscious of the consequences of their actions on the planet."

Another category of answers comes from those who possess what is called "a whole-systems view". Their interpretation is that a mature adult isn't necessarily for or against anything or anyone but will equally favour interventions that foster wellbeing for people and planet, ecology, and economy.

Then there are those who experience themselves as an integral part of the cosmos. They will view a mature adult as someone who regards their own personality as an instrument to be toned, so it can be used for the benefit of the whole.

Each answer is an adequate and potentially wise response to the life circumstances we find ourselves in and the period in our lives. As teenagers we might rebel and reject the ways of our family. Leaving home is a necessary step on the way to adulthood. We may live it up in these unruly years, during which we find out who we are outside of the confines of parental supervision. At some point, as a rule, we cool down, find a job and muster the interest or discipline to be on time and shoulder our responsibilities.

With decisions to make every day, small and big, of momentary and far-reaching consequence, people who become parents put themselves on a fast track towards adulthood. They are responsible for the life of a little one now and so they move up in the ranks of generations. They pick a name that will define a child throughout their life, they pick a school that will help their child unfold their potential, and they pick a place to live. They determine whether to be punitive or permissive and will have to hold the line, because granting one of their brood a favour will have repercussions in the rest of the tribe.

Parents need to learn to hold their tongues and have their chicks find out for themselves if what they are about to do is a wise course of action. They will have to sit on their hands and restrain themselves from speeding up a slow child or organizing for them. They will have to remain open to viewpoints debated with a youthful ardour that are not theirs. If they don't develop some kind of foresight, equanimity, and sagacity, they'll go bonkers.

"I have as much intimacy from family life as I need from being a sister, an aunty, and a great aunty. My community also feels like my family – no blood ties but strong, deep ties with less baggage."

—Woman, 62, educator, Australia

Apart from being bundles of joy, children also are testers of patience, askers of questions, and breakers of rules. Parents live in a relentless house of mirrors that reflect their own conditioning and upbringing. Before they know it, admonitions of their own parents they vowed never to repeat are flying out of their mouths uncensored.

Like us, parents are mirrored at work and through advice of friends or criticism from siblings. No one, however, has less mercy than kids. My sister laughs out loud when she tells me how her youngest (who isn't known for her tact) once looked her up and down, and said, "And you think you're looking good?" Feedback on the fashion front—something we who do not have a 16-year-old in-house stylist at our disposal have to organize for ourselves. I have asked my nieces to let me know when I am wearing clothes too young for my age, and they have pledged to do so.

Apart from fashion advice, we need to organize feedback loops on lots of other terrains, so we don't become too set in our ways or too unworldly.

We need to keep up with technological innovation without a younger generation at hand who seem to be born with skills we are having a hard time mastering. Feedback comes not only from people but also from systems that change, bus routes no longer in service, banks demanding we conduct our business online, laws that are adapted, and customs that declare values different from the ones we've adhered to. If we wish to be wise but not outdated, we must keep innovating and reinventing ourselves and not try to hold onto what once was the norm.

We who have declined parenthood, or to whom this has not been given, need to organize mirrors for ourselves in order to fine-tune the instrument of our personality and develop our sapience. Whereas parents embark on the training that not their will but the baby's will be done the minute their little one is born, we must identify other ways to learn to go with the flow. Whereas parents need to practise standing in their authority when their precious ones test the boundaries again and again and again, we will find our own training grounds at work, in personal development courses, a spiritual practice, or participating in sports that test our limits or improv theatre that requires us to leave our comfort zone. Whereas parents are forced to be authentic, since their children will just make fun of them if they aren't, we peel the onion of acquired beliefs and behaviours to come to the core of our being through self-reflection.

Maybe it is this quality of self-reflection that stands out most in how we develop into mature, authentic, and wise beings in the autumn of our childfree lives. We who have fewer living mirrors in the house have more time on our hands to devote to a conscious path of self-discovery and self-development.

29

Our Parents Revisited

Every one of us, without exception, has gone through the experience of pregnancy and birth. We may not have given birth, but we have been born.

Long before the notion of us existed, thousands of eggs were formed within the ovaries of the embryonic baby who would become our mother. In the first years of our mother's life, most of her eggs were discarded to keep the few hundred that would last her until menopause.

When the one egg that contained half of our chromosomes admitted into itself a determined, fast, spermatozoid swimmer, bringing with it the other 23 chromosomes, we began. We might retain no cognitive memories of our lodging in the womb, yet our cells and our innermost being are forever bonded with this woman who bore us, birthed us, and laid us at her breast. How fearful and frustrated, present and open, nervous and overwhelmed, loving and caring she was with us in our early years will have marked our lives forever.

The bond with our fathers starts on a different footing, as he and we had to forge it from the outside in. He was a stranger at first, looming over our cradle, if he was there at all. Ideally, he provides stability, reassurance, a sense of holding steady. Most parents, alas, are as faulty as the rest of us, and so we have all come out of our childhood wounded and half-grown in aspects we may develop later or choose to ignore.

I go back to psychoanalyst Jeanne Safer. One theme she expands upon in her aforementioned book *Beyond Motherhood* is the relationship the childless women she interviewed had with their own mothers. Their mothers ran the gamut, from loving their traditional housewife role to being free spirits who supported their daughters in making their own choices. Others were immature or antagonistic, jealous or unhappy in their marriage.

"This doesn't mean that forgoing motherhood is primarily reactive or pathological," Jeanne Safer points out. "Women who make this choice often have a highly developed ability to think independently, solid intimate relationships, serious responsibilities, and other indications of maturity and good mental health."

> "As the eldest daughter I have had children since I was 10. My mother died; the girl had to become woman and mother. When I left home at age 23, I literally thought, 'Okay, the children are on their own now.' No hard feelings to anyone, but a lot of space to breathe that I appreciate to this very day as I had to take the mother role so early in life."
>
> —Woman, 57, no occupation stated, the Netherlands

If we are fortunate enough to have our mothers still with us when we ourselves enter the autumnal years, we may continue this most intricate relationship of our lives as a mature adult. We may know our father, know him well. We may have siblings we have known since the day they or we were born. We may have friends from kindergarten and a partner we share long years with, yet none of these relationships compare to the unique one we have with the woman who gave birth to us.

We were once completely dependent upon her for our life. Growing up, we may have felt cherished or trashed by her. We may have rebelled against her, tried to match her, or to live up to her expectations. We might have rejected her, kept her at arm's length, or befriended her. We might have been able to see past our projections once we got older, and vice versa. We may have forgiven her for who she was and for who she was not. We may appreciate her more as our awareness grows of what it takes to raise a child. She may not approve of the way in which we live but, at this age, we no longer need her blessing in order to behave lovingly in our contact with her, anyway. She might begin to need us more as the years progress, and we will need to find the right relationship with her again when we switch caregiver roles.

Several women have spoken to me about the long years it took them to bounce back from the way their mothers treated them. One was a gifted child, who nevertheless could never seem to satisfy her mother. When she graduated, her mother shrugged her shoulders, so she pressed on for a PhD, which she didn't really enjoy. Even that formidable feat was greeted with the implacable question, why didn't she graduate with distinction? This woman found a job on another continent, burying herself in her mind and her work, until she could no longer stand trying to please her mother and realized she had to stand up for herself. She has done her share of therapy and retrained to be a therapist herself. Only now, in her mid-fifties, is she ready for children, so she is on the lookout for a man who has kids already.

I am told stories of mothers who just couldn't do it. They weren't up to the task but only found out after they had brought children into the world. They upped and left to save themselves, leaving their impressionable offspring feeling that they had somehow been the cause of her incomprehensible disappearance.

Only in the autumn of our lives do many of us come to a place of forgiveness and of understanding that it wasn't that we were a pest or a source of despair to our mothers or, worst of the worst, not important enough. Older now and having ripened in our empathy, we may begin to get a sense of how cornered she must have felt in a life not naturally hers, how she must have agonized over the choice to leave, and how she could only have done so in an acute act of self-preservation.

"Now that I am nearing 60, I am finally able to see my mother's side of the story," said a Dutch woman who has raised a child not hers, whom she has not seen since she broke up with the father ten years ago. "Also, I have come to acknowledge how her sudden leaving has set me on a path of fending for myself, which has brought me to where I am. In a weird way, I am coming to a place of gratitude that my mother did what she did, and of admiration for this radical step that must have broken her heart."

Some of us have lives that know a "before" and an "after"—before the divorce and after, when our world fell apart and we had to adjust to being with only one of our parents or travelling between them with our stuff. We had to get along with new partners, perhaps, who stayed in our lives or who kept moving on; with half-siblings, maybe, and the whole rigmarole of composite families.

The "before" and "after" for others was the early death of a parent. In her 1996 classic *The Loss that is Forever,* Maxine Harris, PhD, shows how parental death shatters a child's assumption about how the world works. Drawing on the 66 interviews she conducted, this clinical psychologist describes how the catastrophe crushes core beliefs. A child believes in a safe and secure world that can be understood. If a loved mother or father can disappear overnight, then who knows what other devastating disasters may lie ahead? Harris noted that people who had suffered this type of early loss and were consciously childless named fear of repeating what they had endured as the obvious reason. This fear concerned either their own premature death or losing a child themselves. Harris observes that due to the lack of a role model, some of these adults had never learnt to parent and in a way remained perpetual children.

A Dutch woman in her sixties is at times still flooded by feelings of consternation and powerlessness as a result of losing her mother when she was 14. "I looked at my father," she said, "and saw that he had no clue what to do. When I face difficult situations at work, this early terror sometimes comes out of nowhere: that no one will take care of me, that I am all alone in this world."

Her words echo those of another Dutch woman in her mid-fifties, who lost both of her parents before she turned 17. She, too, has learned how to handle life well but gets panicked when she thinks of her old age. "In the end, life is unsafe. There will be no one to care for me. Story of my life."

Both these women have had to deal with cancer, so they know what they are talking about. When I point out that family and friends stepped forth to drive them to the hospital and accompany them to vital doctor's appointments, they smile and shake their heads. I will find out for myself, I see them think, when my turn comes to be a patient, dependent on others for whom I have not cared in the way parents have cared for their children. Put this way, the old "investment theory" comes back to haunt those of us who have "invested" time in ourselves rather than in offspring who could potentially care for us.

For the time being, however, I find myself not worried. Might this be because I have a partner who is a born caregiver?

I talk this over with a woman in her mid-sixties who would have loved to have had children, who has fully accepted that this wasn't to be for her, who has had two run-ins with cancer, and who lost her partner to heart failure four years ago. Like me, she has more nephews and nieces than the other two women. She enjoys their company, as they do hers, with her probing questions and philosophical outlook on life. Like me, she has had parents who have lived into old age. We both agree that we will cross the bridge of who will be there for us when we are old and frail when we get to it. I do, however, understand that if safety and being looked after are issues due to what occurred in our youth, the sense of a lack of it may come back to haunt us when we get on in years.

> "Over the years, I have spent so much time and energy trying to make sense of my own feelings, circumstances, choices, beliefs, worldview, etc around having children. It was (and is) a lonely journey. It's hard to find others who have had a similar experience and who are willing to talk about it. I think it's a conversation that needs to happen, as societal norms, values, and constructs evolve. The more perspectives, experiences, and ideas that can be shared around this complex topic, the better."
>
> —Woman, 43, organizational coach and consultant, United States

We can evaluate the role of our father, now that we are older than he was when he begot us. He may have been an authority figure, an outsider in the household, an understanding mentor and coach, or someone to shy away from. We may have suffered at his hands or grown under his tutelage. We may have withered under his expectations of who he thought we should be or have risen to meet them. We may have fought with him, physically or emotionally, to get out from under his control, or we may have felt supported in who we could become. He might not have been there much for us at all, having been preoccupied with his own life, his work, or his afflictions. He may have been emotionally available for us, or not. He may have initiated us into his love for nature or stamps or science or booze. He may have coached us or caught us smoking and tried to reason with us or beat it out of us. He may be a figure we despise and strive not to be like or a man we admire and whose counsel we seek, if we are lucky enough to have him still.

With over half a century to look back on, complete with peaks and valleys, we enter a new phase in our relationship with our parents. Hopefully, by now, they will have accepted our decision or life's intervention that we haven't copied the vital part of their existence that gave rise to ours. Our relationship may have been strained when we wouldn't procreate. Together with peers, and society in general, mothers and fathers may have applied pressure or augmented it by favouring siblings who did parent in their wills, in their daily actions, in countless subtle ways of reminding us what we didn't do.

Some of our mothers might unconsciously or secretly have experienced unwarranted feelings of envy of their daughters when we apparently found other role models to emulate. Mothers may have felt jealous of our lives of freedom and self-realization. Fathers may be at a loss as to why their children wouldn't want to follow in their footsteps and continue the lineage. Mothers may have cheered us on as we lived an unfulfilled part of her that she had given up in order to birth us and raise us. Fathers may have been bemused when we trod a path they had not considered or thought a possibility.

If we were not able to conceive, our parents might have been as hard hit as anybody. Not only did they want us to have what they had but they will also not have our children at their knee.

An Englishwoman in her fifties who works in the field of investments to combat climate change told me how difficult it is for her parents—her mother, in particular—to have to reply, "None," when asked how many grandchildren they have. Her mother had always realized and accepted that her eldest daughter's destiny did not lie in having children. The onus, therefore, was on her brother, who found a partner only late in life and then the two of them had a stillborn.

The ensuing trauma and grief and his wife's age prevented them from making another attempt and thus, his parents remained without grandchildren.

An Englishman who grew up on a farm and became a Buddhist monk voices his appreciation at how his parents adjusted their later life plans when his two elder sisters, too, proved to prioritize dedication to their work above family life. "With the three of us stepping out of the 'script', they, too, had to redesign their old age."

A Scotsman comments that he feels sorry that he and his wife have not been able to give his parents grandchildren, as his brother seems keen on remaining single. So these pensioners have no grandchildren, either. One never knows, of course, with men. They can procreate into old age, but by that time, it might be too late for their parents to enjoy little ones of their own flesh and blood.

> "I am a 'sibling', sister to a person with special needs. This played a huge part in my (unconscious) decision not to have children, and I think it's the interesting thing about my story."
>
> —Woman, 52, journalist, Italy

In her beautiful 2013 book *The Faraway Nearby*, one of the stories Rebecca Solnit unpacks is that of organizing and caring for her mother when she disappears into dementia. Her mother calls on her rather than on her brothers, for they are busy with work and family. In her eyes, her daughter just putters around the house, which, the author remarks drily, is one way of describing a writer's life. In this book she weaves stories of arctic explorers and young Mary Shelley's Frankenstein masterpiece together with Che Guevara's visits to leper colonies and her own sojourn in Iceland, all in reflection upon the constant decay in nature, our human bodies and minds included. She explores how we navigate the inevitable end of our days and the illnesses that may lead up to it.

Like no other, this feminist historian describes how we can support each other in times of hardship and pain and increasing practical impossibilities and having to ask. She explores her own predicament of finding she has cancer, having no children to come to her aid, whilst as a daughter she still wants to ease the days of her mother.

When our parents, or one of them, are still alive in this autumnal time of our lives, we are given the opportunity to come full circle in this defining relationship. We may befriend them in the process of dropping our mutual projections and expectations and accepting each other as the person we happen to be. Without the clear demarcation of having produced a member of the next generation, we have some-how also made it to the bank of the adults. The time is not clocked, the moment not marked; ours is a gradual crossing.

30

Thank You, Pioneers

All over Europe, on central squares in our cities and towns, statues have been erected. Proud bronze men sit on their horses, holding the reins of their fiery steeds with one hand, the other pointing to a faraway horizon of enemies to be conquered, lands to be occupied, people to be subjugated, and rewards to be reaped.

All countries have their heroes, who through the changing eye of history may suddenly come to be seen as power-hungry plunderers, thieves, and thugs for their nation, their religion, or their own glory. They do depict men, for the most part, these statues—men who kick history forward, whilst women through the ages have done what they could to keep things together, creating "her-story".

I want to erect statues here for women, for pioneers, for freedom fighters going to battle using words as swords against patriarchal ways that women typically swallowed hook, line, and sinker, until a few clever and determined ones stood up and said, "Wait a minute. Why could I not do what he can do? Why can we not live like they can live?" and made the structure of male supremacy totter.

In acknowledging the many women pioneers who have had the pluck and courage to stand up to a too narrow definition of our female being, I pick four authors—one French, one Australian, and two American, two dead and two still alive.

Their ideas and actions interpreted, and still do, the zeitgeist as it lived through many of us in the last century, whether we read their ground-breaking work or not. They described what we sensed as an indomitable driving power within us, which made us question marriage and the definition of motherhood as the fulfilment of a woman's life. They paved the way for later generations of young women to accept autonomy as a given and to wonder what all the fuss was about.

Betty Friedan

Almost every book by American authors who write on the broad topic of women's lives mentions Betty Friedan and her 1963 bombshell book *The Feminine Mystique*. When attending a reunion of the all-female Smith College, it had struck this former stellar student how dissatisfied many of her peers were. Promising young women once, 15 years after their graduation they were as frustrated in the role of housewife and mother as she was herself, living in New York's suburban Rockland County and raising her three children.

She sent 200 of them a questionnaire with intimate, open-ended questions and interviewed 80. The answers she received confirmed the discrepancy she had already noticed between the happy housewives depicted in ads and magazines and the reality of spending weekdays making beds, shopping for groceries, chauffeuring children, cooking their meals, and laying awake at night, afraid even to ask herself: "Is this all?"

In the many columns, books, articles and films that told women their role was to seek gratification as demure wives and mothers, Betty Friedan had not been able to find a single word on these inner misgivings.

"Over and over," she writes in the introduction to her groundbreaking book, "women heard in voices of tradition that truly feminine women do not want careers. A thousand expert voices applaud their femininity, their adjustment, their new maturity. All they had to do was devote their lives from earliest girlhood to finding a husband and bearing children."

Friedan goes on to debunk the myth of the happy suburban housewife, the dream image, it was said, of young women all over the world.

I have never read this seminal book before, but I am astounded by how accurately Betty Friedan describes my own memories of the time that my mother cherishes as the best part of her life, the years when we as her children really needed her. I find passages that depict conversations I remember having with my mother so accurately it feels uncanny.

In the chapter called "The Forfeited Self", Betty Freidan writes how in our society love has been defined, at least for women, as a complete merging of egos and loss of separateness, a giving up of individuality rather than a strengthening of it.

I travel back in time to a Sunday of lying between my parents in their bed, with my mother telling me how one day I would find a man I would love so much that I would want to merge with him. I remember my face contorting as it does even now when I invoke this memory of over half a century ago and ask in disbelief, "Merge with him?" My mother tried to convey the beauty of the birds and the bees, but I was appalled at the image of losing myself. I certainly never wanted to merge with someone else, I protested.

To this day, I remember how she smiled at my father, shaking her head at me as a daughter who obviously had no idea what life was about.

The next weekend, I asked if we could have this conversation again. As the eldest, I cherished such exclusivity with my parents, finding some of the timeless intimacy we had enjoyed before the others were born. "You didn't have a clue what I was trying to explain to you," my mother maintains.

Maybe I didn't, but I mostly remember my resolve not to disappear into someone else; yet, that definitely was how I was raised. So I hereby erect a statue to this woman who blew the Mad Men and their Bettys out of the water, pointing to a land where women could use an education like the one she received, instead of being cooped up between their appliances.

Simone de Beauvoir

Betty Friedan researched her book a decade after French philosopher Simone de Beauvoir had published *The Second Sex*. In 1946, this French philosopher had sat down to outline what she thought would be an autobiographical essay explaining why the first sentence that came to mind, when she had tried to define herself, was, "I am a woman". Simone de Beauvoir, then a 38-year-old public intellectual in France, went on to write an 800-page encyclopaedia of the way folklore, customs, laws, history, religion, mythology, philosophy, anthropology, literature, and economic systems have, since time began, objectified women.

One needs stamina to read this magnum opus, written in just over one year and long before search engines put such information at anyone's fingertips. The central tenet of this learned tome is that man is the norm and woman is the other. Men are masters of this world, and women are relegated to defining themselves in relation to the forms and norms they create.

This forward thinker described the position of women throughout history up to her own time, when French law no longer included obedience as one of a wife's duties and women could vote, but there was no corresponding economic autonomy. Work, she concluded, could guarantee a woman freedom from being a vassal, even if the world still belonged to men and retained the form they continue to imprint upon it—work and being a sexual person, free to live for herself and by herself, liberated from assimilation, and taking the chance to live her potential.

Many of us will recognize an inner impulse to do just that, even if we have never heard of existentialist philosophy or Simone de Beauvoir. Our mothers may still have brought us up with the notion that we were to make ourselves ready to meet Prince Charming, who would sweep us away to enter the great current of life. Our father would be proud of his daughter's success and the promise of a future with children to repeat the pattern.

Women my age and older, and maybe younger, too, will recognize all of the above in how many of our mothers expected our lives to unfold. I wanted none of it. My father left for work in the morning and came home at his own discretion. Without having the slightest idea of what people in offices did all day, I found his life endlessly more fascinating than that of my mother who in my youthful perception was stuck with us, and the four of us quarreled a lot. Both products of our time, my mother and I quarreled, too. She had started a family without giving it much thought. I could not imagine *not* thinking about how many children there are in the world already, or how my life would irrevocably change and wonder if that was right for me.

It is beyond me as to why there aren't statues on every French village square depicting Simone de Beauvoir, who wrote her feminist masterwork when birth control or abortion were still illegal, when there was no woman head of state anywhere in the world, and girls' role models were limited to fairy princesses, queens who were kept on a short leash, and a handful of scientists and saints. Of course, in France, they do have gilded statues in places of prominence of the indomitable Jeanne d'Arc, but avant-garde Simone de Beauvoir should be honoured at least as much as that other heroine, whose fame reaches mythic dimensions.

> "My mother had eight children and was in an unhappy marriage. I saw her unhappy, feeling trapped, her life force crushed, her options limited, her energy sapped. I think I unconsciously decided to do things differently from an early age. I wanted to travel, experience life all over the globe, have adventures, not be stuck without options."
>
> —Woman, 62, educator, Australia

Gloria Steinem

In her recent memoir, *My Life on the Road*, Gloria Steinem looks back on what drove her to be the leading organizer, activist, writer, and catalyst for change that, now in her eighties, she still is.

She goes into some detail about her itinerant childhood, with her father regularly packing the car to drive the four of them across the United States in search of adventure and ways to make a living.

Planting the seed for a life of travel, this hand-to-mouth existence also instilled in her the concept that being grown-up didn't necessarily mean being tied down in one place. She also spotted at an early age that the life circumstances of certain people didn't seem to matter to the powers-that-be, and how that rubbed her the wrong way. Added to this was the treatment of her mother, who never recovered from a nervous breakdown.

After experiencing the medical profession's hostile attitude towards her mother, Steinem realized that women lacked social and political equality. She became a fearless journalist, following stories of the oppressed and the unseen; a sometime worker in political campaigns; and a tireless feminist organizer working for equality of women and men of colour, of all ages, of all races. In 1972, she co-founded *Ms.* magazine, which advocates women's rights across the globe. She continues to have hope and energy to protest on behalf of what she believes in, she says, because she still travels and listens to stories that are very different close up than from a safe distance.

She has spent her life on the road, so where would her statue be? In front of the *Ms.* offices might be a logical spot, but I bet she would want it somewhere more adventurous, not in bronze but as an assemblage of debris in Syria or as a beacon in the Mediterranean for refugees to hold onto.

Germaine Greer

In 1970, Australian Germaine Greer burst on the scene in the United Kingdom with her book *The Female Eunuch*. Her provocative thesis was that men hate women, and that unaware of this, women are taught to hate themselves. Not one to mince words, this academic denounced the traditional suburban, consumerist, nuclear family as systematic sexual repression of women that strips away their vitality, making them into the equivalent of eunuchs.

With her unruly hair, her forays into film (in which she often appeared naked), and her irreverent speech, Germaine Greer was a frequent speaker on talk shows and panels. Invariably, she would shock her interviewer or her audience with her scholarly polemics and her attitude of not needing to be liked, if only she could get the point across that it was time for revolution. Women, in her view, should get to know and accept their bodies, taste their menstrual blood, and enjoy their sexuality.

Germaine Greer has lost nothing of her directness as she continues to fight for freedom for women to have dignity, pride, and passion. She still encourages women not to be afraid to speak up and run and love the earth with all that swims, lies, and crawls upon it. Before the recent royal wedding that millions enjoyed as a star-studded spectacle, she advised American Meghan Markle on national television to grab Prince Harry and run for her life.

A first statue for this freedom fighter might be erected in her beloved county of Sussex. I wouldn't be surprised, though, if she would rally against such nonsense or come to paint it with blood on the day after its unveiling, which she of course would not attend.

31

My Autumn

The first time I spoke to friends about experiencing bouts of depression, I was in my forties and they wouldn't believe me. "We all have our bad days," they said, with a knowing smile. But they knew nothing of the months of darkness, the weekends when I would lie in bed without moving so I wouldn't hurt so much; the inner crying and despair that went on 24/7; or my fantasies of killing myself by roping stones around my waist and jumping into a canal, with only the technicalities of which rope and stones to use and how to do it without anyone noticing remaining unsolved.

It has these days become apparent that millions suffer from depression—maybe always have, as in the past it was called by different names: the blues, despondency, a hard patch, glumness, melancholia.

When I was 15, my parents didn't know anything about the phenomenon and were at a loss for a term to describe my disconsolate state. As I had just learned about the gloom of Robert Schumann in music class, they called my dark mood by that composer's name. "Ah, you're Schumann again," my mother would say when I came home from school crying, day after day. Try as she might to cheer me up and distract me from my misery, her geniality would merely invoke in me contempt at the superficial nature of life, with the result that I dug an ever deeper pit for myself.

My mother was overjoyed when I went to study in Leiden, where she expected me to meet the man whose love would end my inclination towards the dark. I wasn't nearly as astute as the pioneers honoured in the previous chapter. Thinking that maybe if I did indeed adapt and conform to what everyone around me seemed to enjoy I would get rid of the big black wolf, I plunged into student life and later started my own business.

For years, I fooled my friends by being active and appearing upbeat, whilst inside, I despaired at the state of the world, the numerous wars in spite of our supposedly "being developed", and the meaningless-ness of life, in general, and mine in particular.

No wonder they wouldn't believe me, when I first told them I suf-fered from bouts of depression lasting five to eight months, two winters out of three. I had played my part of happy not-housewife so convincingly I had prevented them from noticing.

After opening up to these friends, I confided in many more, and in Jos, my partner, whom I had just met. His trained painter's eye started to see patterns in my behaviour. He could spot the black cloud the moment I opened my eyes in the morning and addressed this inner weather condition as soon as it appeared and helped to dispel it.

Having just sold my business and not having unruly teenagers to look after, I was free to explore what I was going to do next. I went to the Findhorn Foundation in Scotland, where I found the outer mani-festation of my inner world in the spiritual community that would for the next 20 years become my home away from home.

I enrolled in the Barbara Brennan School of Healing in the United States for four years to obtain a BSc in energy healing. I compare that esteemed training institution to a chimney sweep, as I was taught the tools of releasing old pains and limiting beliefs. Having learnt the magic of working consciously with energy, I opened a private practice in the Netherlands

> "I love children. I enjoy spending time with them and then giving them back to their parents. There are a lot of logical reasons I could give for not wanting family—addiction and mood disorders run in my family, the world is scary, I never had a partner who wanted kids, but really, I just never wanted to be a mother."
>
> —Woman, 49, home organizer and chef, United States

For a dozen years, I thought I was freed from depressions forever, but I have had to let go of that story, too. They are not as deep as they were, though, when I possessed none of the tools of self-tracking and attunement to the eternal peace of Spirit. I have come to know that I go down the slippery slope when I try to force myself to do something that seems right but that isn't right for me. It's the film reel again, whose bandwidth allows me only so much room to move, and which brings boundless energy and joy when I stay within its light.

32

A One-on-One Relationship

One woman I talked to in Switzerland had originally married her best friend, and the two of them were always busy with their lives—getting the boat in order for summer, sailing all through the season, having the boat repaired, fixing their house up, going skiing as often as they could in winter. Their conversations, their whole existence, were about doing this and that and the next thing. They both had careers, and it all looked good, yet it slowly dawned on her that being together needed more than friendship, and she was not going to have children with her husband-friend.

Then, one day at work, Cupid shot his arrow as she entered a meeting and a new colleague was introduced to her. She had always cherished her young girl's dream of an all-encompassing love, and here he was now.

Her second husband of seven years—and lover for longer—has no children either. His first wife had been demanding. She wanted the house, the art, the friends in high circles, and the money to spend. He delivered it all. When it came to children, though, he drew a line in the sand.

When the two of them first got together, they could still have tried for children; yet, with almost two decades between them and wanting to disentangle themselves from their respective marriages with grace, they chose not to. "In the end," they say, seeking each other's hands and eyes, "we wanted to maximize our time together."

"My husband had had a vasectomy which, although reversed in an operation, did not work. I considered leaving him, but the drive to have children was not strong enough to leave a man whom I loved."

Woman, 60, director of a social enterprise, United Kingdom

On their 11th wedding anniversary, Laura Carroll and her husband found themselves looking to the future. They loved each other and were enjoying the life they had created together but wanted to learn from the road maps of other long-married couples who had chosen not to parent. Not finding any books on happily married couples without children by choice, Laura Carroll decided she would write one herself. She advertised in newspapers and magazines and was soon flooded with calls and emails from couples who met the criteria.

Her 2000 book *Families of Two* contains 15 of the interviews she conducted. She started out asking family and friends if they could introduce her to couples who were childless by choice and married for at least ten years without either of them having children from a previous liaison. She advertised in newspapers and magazines and was soon flooded with calls and emails from couples who met the criteria.

When she told her mother about her book project, at first her mother was shocked and told her she could not tell any of her friends about her daughter's book. This reaction led to a heartfelt discussion between the two of them. Her mother confessed she had wondered about her role in her daughter's choice not to have children, and her daughter expressed how thankful she was to have been raised to believe she could create the life she wanted and live in her own way.

The in-depth interviews with the 15 couples in their homes on key questions about their life without children show there is no one road map to a good lifelong marriage without children.

Learning from the couples she interviewed inspired the author and her husband to continue creating a marital road map that is all their own, which includes consciously cultivating their relationship and valuing the time they have to do this.

Part of a purposeful life for this author involves "mothering" the creative process, becoming "pregnant" with information, and "midwifing" words into the "birth" of a new creation that may bring inspiration to others.

Like many of the couples interviewed, the author and her husband don't model traditional gender roles. They bought a mountain cabin, where they live for three months of the year. They have a mix of friends, some with children, some without. At age 40, her husband changed career. These two consciously cultivate their relationship and value the time they have to do this.

I recognize this. At least once a week, Jos and I remark to one another how blessed we feel that we have time to spend together, just the two of us. We also make a point of doing just that, visiting places we both enjoy or sitting silently at home, each on a couch with our own books and then cooking our favourite dishes for dinner.

When I look around, I see the glue between childless couples made up of a mix of love, deep mutual appreciation, shared interests, and pleasure in being together without necessarily doing anything together. As friends of mine who are soon to celebrate their 25th wedding anniversary said, "On the weekend, we putter around the house in our PJs, each to our own, and have the best of times."

I know quite a few other couples, who are a joy to be with in their bliss of having found one another in their first or second rounds of childless unions. With no other reason to stay together than wanting to, they exude felicity and wellbeing. They are open and interested in what happens in the worlds of culture and politics, the environment, and the spiritual. Most of all, maybe, the glue contains a staunch support of each other to keep pursuing new avenues to find fulfilment.

Many say that they feel as close as they are because there is no third person. "We are all about us," as my PJ friends joyfully stated.

33

Children in Our Lives

I t's hardly ever all about us. In the 70 interviews I held for this book, only two persons stated that they didn't actively seek friendship with the younger generation outside their family. All others had found younger friends along the way and consciously kept such contacts alive.

A former teacher made friends with five young women in her various classes who now regularly come to dinner and seek her and her husband's counsel. "All young people should have an extra adult in their lives," she theorizes.

Conversely, as we grow older we need to be around youngsters. The husband in my PJ friends had a previous long-term relationship with a woman who had a son. He never acted as the father, but after the break-up with the mother he did make a point of attending the boy's birthdays and subsequent major life event celebrations. Now he is regarded as a surrogate grandfather to this young man's child, which is a role he enjoys playing.

Many of us inherit children from the previous relationships of partners, whilst we ourselves have none. Especially when the children are still young, the role of a stepparent isn't always easy. We are not their mothers or fathers, so we have no right to speak when we feel lines of suitable behaviour are being crossed. This is not only how many children feel and act in these relationships; in most countries around the globe, a stepparent is a legal alien with no rights what-soever over the children, even if they clothe and feed them on a day-to-day basis.

Sweden and Canada hold the broadest, most accepting views of family. Australia, which dedicates national resources to help its sizable stepfamily population, comes in third. In the United States, stepparents in most cases have no legal rights or obligations towards their stepchildren. Mexico doesn't provide any legal support for stepfamilies, and in general ignores the issue. Even if a good part of its population holds traditional views on family roles, Argentina has developed legal precedents for legitimizing the stepparent-stepchild relationship, whilst retaining all parental rights and responsibilities. In New Zealand, too, stepfamily relationships have been institutionalized, and stepparents have legal decision-making rights alongside biological parents.

The underlying conundrum for all countries is deciding who is "kin" and who is not. "Establishing roles and a sense of family identity calls for tolerance of uncertainty and ambiguity," according to Jan Pryor, who contributed to and assembled *The International Handbook of Stepfamilies*, one of the only global collections of stepfamily research.

> "I thought I would have children, but my first husband and I divorced. Then I got involved with someone who already had children. I struggled for a while with wanting children, then chose the relationship over becoming a parent. Seventeen years later we are still together, very close as we live and work together."
>
> — Woman, 50, interfaith minister, United Kingdom

When we fall in love with someone who has children from a previous relationship, we get into a situation where some sort of trauma has happened. Some split families may have found a new rhythm that works well for all involved, whereas others might be struggling in the aftermath for years on end. Even if the divorce was friendly, something must have given rise to it, and children have often felt this long before the parents decided to take the step to separate and part ways.

As the new person in the mix, we have not been through the quarrels and fights or the coldness and indifference preceding the divorce of our newfound love. How we negotiate our way into the hearts of the children of our new partner depends on us as much as it depends on the age of the offspring at the time we enter the scene and the attitude of our beloved. Those of us who have not particularly wanted children may hold an advantage over those who have fervently hoped to be a parent one day. The latter may want to occupy a place in the heart of the child that it is not ready to offer, while the former may be content to live as a surrogate parent in the practical sense without ever truly becoming one or needing to be given that place.

On blog forums, I read one post after the other from women who have a hard time with their stepchildren. They spend the better part of their precious holidays with their partners' children and feel like the odd one out. Resentment builds and they offload on forums where others recognize their plight.

"Talk to your partner," unknown friends reply.

"Why can't he see what he is doing?", the indignant stepmother fumes.

"You must make him see," is the advice given, "and make sure you go on a trip together soon, just the two of you. Good luck!"

Others might have had the children on a more daily basis, got them out of bed in the morning, driven them to play dates or sports fields in the afternoon, fed and helped with their homework in the evening, and worried about them at night. Then, when Mother's Day came around, the children made clumsy cards for their mother and didn't for a minute think about the other one who cared for them. Women who gave up on having children of their own because their new partner didn't want to start a second family, talk of their pain over performing all the maternal tasks yet not being treated as a mother on that day, or on many others. Member posting boards on specialized websites like Steps for Stepmothers are filled with posts entitled "Fed up and need to vent" and "How do you handle manipulation?"

With a PhD in comparative literature, Wednesday Martin began researching her 2009 book *Stepmonster* six years into marrying a man with kids from a previous partnership.

Over and over, people with stepparents told her that they liked their stepdads just fine, even considered them "another dad". Their stepmoms, they insisted, were the problem. More often than not, they called her "my father's new wife". Most notable was the marked frequency of strained relations between stepdaughters and stepmothers. The author found research that corroborated her findings that most women took on life with a man with kids of any age with the best of intentions, often bending over backwards to try to win over his wary brood.

> "I have a 23-year-old stepdaughter whom I have known since she was 10. I am very grateful to know her and play a role in her life. And that we had her half the time only. Wonderful to have the other half of the week for the two of us. From time to time her half-sister, who is 10 years her junior and not related to us, also comes to stay, which I enjoy. It gives me an opportunity to live my maternal side. And I am also delighted when she returns home again . . . ;) Pffff, quite exhausting, children."
>
> —Woman, 41, trainer/coach/author, the Netherlands

In an article she wrote for *Psychology Today*, Wednesday Martin cites retired psychology professor Mavis Hetherington, a pioneer explorer of family dynamics who conducted a 20-year longitudinal study of divorce and remarriage, following 450 families in Virginia. One of her findings was that stepmothers are frequently singled out for bad treatment by stepchildren, who pick up on their mother's anger and become her proxy in expressing disdain for their father's new partner. In such cases, it greatly helps if the mother gives the child explicit permission to like the stepmother and lets it be known that being nasty to Stepmom is not an option.

Wednesday Martin herself warns against feeling compelled to try and win a partner's kids over. "This too often includes trying to act maternal and loving," she maintains. "For a young or adult child such attempts 'to act like she's my mom' will seem offensive and threatening. Thus the stepmother will be more roundly rejected."

Not all is misery in stepmotherland. I have spoken to women who feel that the addition of his children to their lives is an enrichment that all navigate well, whilst they themselves are also able to spend time with their new man and pursue a career without the trappings of having to do full-time caring. They leave his children mostly to him.

Others come into the lives of the children at a later stage, when these children have left home, or are about to. Some children are mature enough to not begrudge their parents a new love life and are clear that they appreciate the new partner but don't need an extra parent. One of my friends reports that very soon into the relationship, she was the one maintaining the contact with his offspring. At his funeral not long ago, his children explicitly honoured her for having been the glue that kept them together.

If separation and divorce of parents cast long shadows, the intensity of the death of one of their parents is even stronger. I have seen from close quarters how children, even if they are young adults, are perennially imagining the response, advice, loving arms of their mother or father, missing them greatly, even as their image unforgivingly fades over time.

Whoever enters the life of a partner with children who have lost their other parent sets foot in a world of pain and smashed trust in life. Such a stepparent will have to tread carefully. At the same time, free from the heartrending pain that has torn through this family, they might actually be the ones who keep life going and who can provide a sense of stability and faith in the future.

> "I 'adopted' two brothers, now seven and eight years old, as my grandchildren, and this is a great joy and gift in my life!"
>
> —Woman, 59, spiritual psychologist and creative career coach,
> the Netherlands

For some entering into a relationship with someone who already has children is a dream come true. A friend of mine in Scotland protests when I call him for a chat about not having children.

"But I have children," he says.

"But they're not yours," I counter.

"But they feel like mine," he argues.

He was the eternal bachelor until he met his match and married at age 50. He has had to adapt to having three teenagers in the house instead of the lone silence he was used to. Now he cannot imagine his life without these young people who have since left home and are finding their way in the world.

"They go around claiming that they have four parents, as their father is also in a new relationship," he says cheerfully.

He also confides to me something we had never spoken about in all our years of friendship and working together, which is that he had long yearned for the fulfilment of fatherhood. Sure, he finds it a challenge to put the needs of others before his own, especially when they were all living together, but he is delighted to have had that experience. He feels well rounded, now that this part of him has also been brought to life.

More than a few people tell me about the joy that grandchildren bring to them after having never been a parent. They came into the lives of their partner's children, when the dust of the divorce had settled and the children were well on their way to adulthood. They never assumed a role in the lives of these near-adults other than "the new partner of".

In many cases, this brought a palpable relief to the children, as it enabled them to release their anxiety of "what to do with Mum or Dad over Christmas". A secular miracle, as a Dutch author called it, happens when one of these children gives birth. Overnight, without ever having been a parent, a grandparent is born. For some men and women, this is an ideal role that brings lots of opportunities to enjoy the rapture of new life without needing to assume direct responsibilities.

An American man who never wanted children says that he loves being seen as a granddad by the grandchildren of his partner of the past 15 years. With their own dad missing, he has been jumping in to provide both financial and practical support.

The aforementioned Dutch author tells me how their first grand-child came to stay when he was one and a half years old. She made a bit of a thing out of stating that, yes, she was delighted to be his grand-mother, but she wasn't going to change his poo-filled nappies. She had never performed this task in her life, and wasn't going to start now. A girl was born two years later, and although the children unre-servedly consider her their grandmother, they are old enough now to work out that she is not the mother of their mother or their father. When she jokes that a good trait of theirs must certainly hail from her, they wrinkle their noses for a moment before shouting out merrily that what she says is, of course, totally impossible.

This wise woman has set a few other boundaries. She never has the children to stay at their house. They rent a cabin or go camping, but no kids on her childfree turf unless accompanied by the parents. She might put in some babysitting, if she has time on her hands, but mostly she leaves that to her husband who, with his first wife, divides the grandparenting duties amicably between them.

34

The Big M

It seemed such a good idea at the time. Soon after her 1970s, hippy-style wedding, Marcia Drut-Davis is the astonished recipient of expectant looks and suggestive comments from her mother-in-law. She and her husband have never discussed children, and her secret is that she doesn't really want them.

She believes she is surely the only woman on the planet who has entertained this strange idea, until her stepmother sends her *The Baby Trap* by Ellen Peck. Her young husband reads the book, too, and voices his relief, as he has never wanted children, either. The book lists the telephone number of an organization for non-parents. She calls. And her life will never be the same again, she writes in her 2013 memoir *Confessions of a Childfree Woman*.

She becomes involved in the now defunct, then cutting-edge organization, where they meet people from all kinds of backgrounds who have also made the choice not to parent. They discuss the disparity between the way people react to the childfree compared with those with children. Whoever they tell they don't want children feels free to ask them why, whereas it would be considered an affront if they in turn asked why the other people did have kids. They query why in all of their education they have never heard that parenting is a choice, not a requirement.

Having become active participants in the group, the couple is asked if the two of them would be prepared to appear on national television as part of a *60 Minutes* segment on people who decide to remain childfree. They hatch a plan to record the conversation of the husband telling his parents about their choice, and on that fateful day in 1974, with the camera crew having turned the apartment into a studio, they break the news to his parents that they are not going to have grandchildren.

His father's face turns to stone. His mother fights her tears. The two of them stare at the young couple, who can no longer find the words that came so easily when they sat with their like-minded friends. The parents start to hammer away at them, telling them that they will regret their decision—they will be lonely and miserable in their old age, just as they themselves will be now that their son has made the selfish choice not to continue the family tree.

"What did we do wrong in raising you," they wail, with the cameras ruthlessly rolling, "and where, pray, would you be, if we had thought along the same lines?"

The segment, entitled "Three's a crowd," airs a few months later, on Mother's Day. The host, Mike Wallace, announces how more and more people are choosing not to start a family. He sets the stage by voicing doubts as to whether this is smart or simply selfish. The whole conversation with the bewildered parents turns out to have been cut to three miserable minutes, during which the young pair was shown having trouble expressing themselves coherently and the parents looked crestfallen.

The next morning, Marcia Drut-Davis does not receive a single teacher substitute request; nor does she receive any the day after. As it turns out, after the nationwide exposure, schools are loath to hire her—she must be a child hater, after all.

An astute woman, who loves teaching, she goes on to become a guest speaker at high schools on the choice of whether or not to parent. She gets hateful reactions from neighbours and friends but praise from teachers keen to avoid teenage pregnancies. Over time, she goes back to teaching, divorces her husband, and marries again.

She confesses to having had spells of regret that she has never experienced the grateful hug of a child, the pride of a parent and the evolution of her baby into a mature adult. When she goes into menopause, her new husband reiterates to her how happy he is in their family of two with their dog. She begins to see that, although many a mother deplores the end of their baby-making years, she is actually happy to enter into her post-periods phase.

Other women I interviewed said the same. They are in their late forties, and they didn't want children or didn't have the partner to want them with, but they still could, if they really wanted. The door isn't closed, until the big M hits.

They are perturbed when the media go overboard about celebrities getting pregnant at the latest possible hour. The eager publicity about them and their adorable babies gets thoughts of late motherhood going again. They pine for the years of choice that got extended and extended over the course of their lives. If only menopause would come, they would be freed of these wretched periods with its characteristic pains that didn't serve them anyway.

"What a delight to be free of these speculations," one of them says. With her partner of almost 20 years, she had decided not to go for a family. After they split up, he soon had a child with his next woman friend. She and her friends can't wait to cross the fertility line.

"I am looking forward to the next phase of life in which I don't need precautions to have sex and don't need to fret about whether I will have a baby or not. I will remain childless. Period."

35

Taking Our Losses

At the funeral of her partner of 35 years, my friend came in with her arms around two of her teenage grandchildren. During the service, her two children flanked her, with her son putting his arm around her from time to time. Towards the end, her husband's two granddaughters and her five grandchildren, who all called him by the same sweet grandfatherly name, stood in a semicircle around his casket.

When they each spoke a sentence of what he had meant to them, it occurred to me that this funeral was a vertical affair. We were sitting next to his brothers, who didn't play a role in the funeral proceedings. My bereaved friend had her children and his children and their grandchildren around her, just as they had clustered around her partner in the months of his decline and the weeks of him entering into the process of dying.

I speak of this verticality with my sister and say, "When Jos dies…" and before I can go on, she jumps in and finishes my sentence, "we will sit next to you."

This moves me to tears, and we talk about how I share events on our family WhatsApp while she predominantly shares in her own family's group. I already go horizontal, whereas she tends to go vertical. Even after all these years, even with my 100 percent happiness that I have honoured my path, I feel a tinge of shame as we speak—as if it is somehow dishonourable and awkward to need my siblings instead of having produced a tribe of my own to lean on when old age comes along with all its inevitable trappings.

A gay friend shared with me years ago what he dreaded most about his single childfree life. It was the notice of his death in the newspaper, he said, with his brothers and their children as the undersigned. He pictured how his lonely name with only connections through the horizontal plane would not do justice to the fullness of his life. He would like to convey to unknown people who scrutinize those death notices, piecing lives together from the sparse information, how his life suited him, how he has loved and lost and overcome, and come to love no matter what.

> "Being 60 now, I regret more than ever not having children, and now no grandchildren, either. I try to keep enough friends, but am anxious and terrified looking ahead to a lonely old age."
>
> —Woman, 60, journalist, the Netherlands

We start to lose friends and partners in the autumn of our lives, and if we haven't before, this is also the season in which many of us lose our parents or the one we still have.

They will need our help in these final years, as we needed theirs in our first ones. When their memory starts to fail, when their legs don't do what they used to, when they cannot master new systems online, we need to be their legs, their memory, and their devices for them.

An American woman relates how her siblings were both too busy with their own families and too aggravated by her mother to come to her side when she became terminally ill. Being single and without children, she stepped in. Increasingly, over the 17 months in which she was the main caregiver, she became the mother of the mother who had disowned her when she was still in high school.

"I wanted her to die knowing she was loved," says this woman in her early fifties. "So I made sure that she was warm and fed, that her needs were met, that she didn't feel abandoned, and that my siblings talked to her over the phone at least."

In this period, the estranged mother met her grandchildren for the first time. Her eldest daughter wouldn't visit. Her son, whom she had not seen since he was 20, wanted to meet her only once. My friend put her personal life on hold for this woman who had birthed her and not been there for her when she grew up, and the mother was lucky to have her.

Not all parents who scorn us for not having children will find their own children as devoted to them at the end of their days. Yet, as we who have no children grow older, the question starts to loom as to who will look after us when we need care, who will sit with us when we are lonely, who will keep our life going when we are no longer able to organize ourselves.

As a Dutch religious worker who recently retired put it, "Who will look after my affairs when I vanish into Alzheimer's?" Her health is not what it used to be, and she has not found an easy answer to this poignant question yet.

Her conclusion is that the final part of our life is not easy, especially being single and childless and in search of new occupations, a new identity really, now that she can no longer derive one from her work. With her reflective nature, she does, however, take pleasure in witnessing how she and others in the same boat cope, which inner strengths will turn out to be helpful, how faith will prove to be the avenue for keeping up her spirits.

With the growing number of ageing people without children, new solutions need to be found across the board. Pondering her question, I have a proposal along the lines of the variety of child benefits and family allowances that many countries have in place.

Canadian parents, for instance, are subsidized with a higher amount in the first five years of a child's life, whereas in Finland and the Netherlands, the annual amount grows with the age of the child. Australians can claim a fortnightly payment through the income tax system, and the United Kingdom gives parents a weekly amount, which is markedly higher for the firstborn than for the children that follow. Ireland makes no distinction in age or number of children but extends the benefit to those in full-time education. South Korea recently decided to provide benefits to parents of children for the first six years, excluding only the top 10 percent richest families. Belgium offers supplementary benefits depending on the social status of a parent, while the Czech Republic, Italy,

Lithuania, Russia, and Singapore offer a child benefit to be spent on housing, education, health care, or a mother's pension. In the Netherlands, the quarterly child benefits are raised twice, at the ages of six and 12, and finish at age 18 when other regulations come into place for those who continue their education.

My proposal is for an end-of-life allowance modelled on existing baby benefits or family allowances for "solo agers", as seniors who are single, divorced, or widowed without children have come to be described. Such a plan will need some hard-nosed lobbying with politicians and policy makers by organizations focused on elderly issues, such as Age UK in Britain and AARP in the United States.

My vision is for this allowance to be paid out to solo agers from, say, age 75, or earlier if our health starts to fail us. If we receive the equivalent of what parents in our respective countries have been paid, we need worry no more about who will look after our affairs when we are no longer able to do so. We can afford to have someone come in and do it for us.

36

The Issue of Regret

I am inclined to encourage young people, who seriously entertain the idea of childless living to stick to their guns, but several peers give different advice.

"You should warn them off, not cheer them on," says one acquaintance with some consternation. She is a friend of a friend, who like me has never made choices that led to having children. "Young people cannot possibly foresee how the choice not to have children will work out for them. This decision has myriad unforeseen consequences."

She is not only talking about potential regrets people might have once it is too late. As a woman who, after two intense relationships, has mostly been on her own, she warns against "an invisible life". With her soft, almost girlish features, she takes me by surprise with her vehemence.

"When I stop working, I will have nothing to show for myself," she argues, hitting the sofa with her hand. "What I have devoted my time and energy to will become invisible, just like my life is invisible to most of my friends who have children. Because I have no parenting experience, they discount my wisdom. I get told off when I try to contribute my insights into parental dilemmas. 'You don't know what it is like,' they tell me. As if I have not been a keen observer of the various ways in which they go about raising their offspring."

She stops to see if I am taking in what she is saying, then continues.

"Having no children, we're always holding the short end of the stick. Years ago, when we rented a house on the beach with my whole family, my teenage nieces were given one of the big bedrooms. I was assigned a single room in the attic. No one blinked an eye, and I knew that if I protested, I would only have lost brownie points, so I gritted my teeth and complied. Now these nieces have become mothers, so they are treated like queens, and I remain the slightly weird solo aunt. Sure, they like to have me around, but my opinions hold no sway, and all the attention is on the next generation."

She repeats, "You must warn young people. They cannot know how their perception on being childless will change or how vulnerable they will feel in later years."

Again, she fixes her gaze on me. Do I get what she means?

I do, but what she feels so strongly isn't my experience. Especially in this later season of life, I actually feel less vulnerable than many of the parents I know. Some of their children are struggling to get their lives together, are depressed, or going through an ugly divorce. Several of these women are hurt because they do not get to see their grandchildren, because their in-laws don't like them or the young family pretends that they are too busy or live too far away to visit. For others, births of grandchildren come with grief for babies lost and agony for what their children must go through.

One of my friends has a daughter who desperately wants another child after the miracle of the first one, which arrived after a number of late miscarriages. My friend's life is not only overshadowed but, to my eyes, determined by the cycles of this daughter's moons, conceptions, and losses. In addition, another daughter has come back to live with her, due to unexplained health issues that prevent her from taking care of herself.

Many people my age become hugely involved in the lives of their children and grandchildren, regularly helping out with babysitting, doing laundry, or shopping. They love it, I can tell, but nature is kind, so we who have never had children don't truly know what that feels like.

A sign of these times is the growing voice of women who openly acknowledge that they regret motherhood. French psychoanalyst Corinne Maier stoked an international media storm in 2007, when she published her booklet *No Kids: 40 Good Reasons NOT to Have Children.*

Generally speaking, people have children for the wrong reasons, she professes. They are afraid of being alone and want to grasp a tiny bit of immortality, but parents are doing something very foolish, just because they have believed something that is not true. Her "good reasons" not to have children range from "You avoid becoming a walking pacifier" and "Open the nursery, close the bedroom" to "Your kid will always disappoint you."

As tends to happen, when someone puts their finger on what is alive in the substratum of our collective psyche, the book quickly spawned articles in newspapers and magazines worldwide. One after another, women stepped forward to speak of the mistake they felt they had made in becoming a mother.

In 2016, another controversial book on the topic, *Regretting Motherhood*, saw the light of day. Doctor of sociology and social activist Orna Donath conducted a study of mothers who regretted having had children in her native Israel, a country where, on average, a woman gives birth to three children.

"We already know that motherhood can be a meaningful relationship that instils feelings of fulfilment, joy, love, comfort, pride, and satisfaction," she explained in her introduction about why she had conducted this study. "At the same time, motherhood can be saturated with tensions and ambivalence that might create helplessness, frustration, guilt, shame, anger, hostility, and disappointment." She wanted to examine if language could be found for these hidden feelings mothers must surely have.

Her respondents have each chosen a pseudonym, since it was deemed unwise to come out in the open naming feelings like the following: "I'm a mother whose children are important to her; I love them, I read books, I get professional counseling, I try to do my best to give them a better education and a lot of warmth and love. . . But still, I hate being a mother. I hate this role. I hate being the one who has to place boundaries, the one who has to punish. I hate the lack of freedom, the lack of spontaneity. The fact that it restricts [me], that this is it. . . ."

The #regrettingmotherhood hashtag went viral on social media as soon as the book was published. Orna Donath was an immediate must-have guest on talk shows worldwide and a new generation of regretting mothers was inspired to come out of the closet.

One of them is Sarah Fischer, mother of a two-year-old daughter. The title of her book in her adoptive German language would translate to *The Mother Bliss Lie.* The subtitle *Why I Would Rather Have Become a Father* alludes to the fact that the author feels professionally and personally limited as she is involuntarily pushed into the classic mother role.

Fischer, a television producer and experienced travel guide in Mongolia, wishes only the best for her daughter Emma. Most especially she wishes for her that culture catches up with the needs and qualities of women; that nothing in her life will change when she becomes a mother one day; that she can continue to live as she did and be a mother. As Fischer perceives most fathers do.

On the public Facebook page "I Regret Having Children", which was started in 2012 and now has over 10,000 followers, people post (typically anonymously) about their regrets, fatigue, financial worries, being sold into marriage, being too young or too old to have had a child, children with severe special needs, hating their life, and wishing they could turn back time.

A woman in her fifties wonders if regrets can also come later in life. She has them now. Her children barely speak to her and only seem to remember those times when she lost her cool as a single mom, which she was during most of their childhood. She resents them fiercely for this. "I don't like spending time with them," she writes on this page that wishes to let mothers and fathers know that regretting parenthood is not abnormal and shouldn't be a taboo subject. "I don't like the adults my children have become. I regret deeply being their mother or being a mother altogether. I feel cheated."

Regrets go both ways, and this is not the final word about them; but at least words can be typed on anonymous forums these days, where the depths of despair can be voiced and recognized by others and solace found.

37

Time on Our Hands

When our working years are behind us, we have to shape our life anew. There are no grandchildren to look after for us, except perhaps when we have acquired them through our partner or through having become an extra in the life of other young people.

Old friends might resurface from their busy two-track lives of family and work. We may find ourselves spending time together like we used to, before the road forked and they went one way and we the other. This will only be a mutual pleasure, though, when they are not preoccupied with the wellbeing and, worse, unquestioned fabulousness of their offspring, which they wish to tell us all about.

Health permitting, we may wish to spend our time volunteering in various ways—on boards that draw on our expertise, in churches that welcome our devotion, or perhaps in organizations that connect us to youngsters who have no grandparents of their own to spend time with.

We may take lifelong learning seriously and embark on a course of study at university or through reading on our own. If we are single, this period of growing into eldership will demand more than ever that we are self-starters who continue to put energy into mingling. We will need the quality of being self-directed more than ever, for it is now up to us to keep going, even as the external structures of work and engagement, which provided content and contacts, fall away.

In our late sixties and early seventies, when we begin to move a bit slower and need a tad more time to get ourselves going, the quality of being self-sufficient will support us by helping us find continuing pleasure in what has always brought a smile to our lips, such as a plant that flowers, a book that entertains or informs, or a visit with friends who talk not so much about the good old times but rather about what is of interest today in local or national politics, in popular culture, in gardens, art, or architecture.

Some of us will find that our professional opinions or skills continue to be sought after, and that we can supplement our pension, if we have one, by still earning our keep.

After choosing to downsize her life to make the most of her remaining time with her ailing husband, a Canadian friend who is now over 70 is publishing her third book on sustainable cities and is in the process of writing her fourth. After his death, she moved to the Findhorn Foundation community and eco-village. Following her husband's demise she gave most of her late husband's possessions to his children, her own to neighbours and friends, and anything left over went to a charity shop. What she wanted to keep, she shipped off to Scotland or packed away in boxes and put in long-term storage for her return, whenever that will be.

I know others, too, who might not be as adventurous as she is but still work well into their seventies, or as long as their health permits.

> "I would have liked to have had children with my second husband, but they didn't arrive. Although for a certain period this led to disappointment, looking back I'm very happy with the life I'm living, which would probably not have been possible if I had had children."

—Woman, 57, singer and community networker, Germany

The topic of ageing and all it brings with it creeps into our conversations. Who amongst us has made a will and if so, can they give tips on how to go about that? What do we think about medically prolonging life? We may try to dodge the subject by joking that we still look 50, but pitying glances will tell us all we need to know: the time has come to face the facts and do some planning of our own so we don't burden others.

Some may have taken steps already to sort out their affairs whilst still of sound mind and body and downsizing our clutter while our muscles can still handle heavy lifting. The attic, the cellar, or an extra room may be full of stuff we were once delighted to acquire and haven't looked at for ages. We may need to force ourselves to get rid of that pasta machine we never mastered, the records we have no player for anymore, or the books turning to dust on our shelves.

Not all of our precious collections of whatnots will be of interest to others, but we may begin to give away beloved possessions. This, of course, brings the benefit of seeing the joy (hopefully) on the face of the chosen beneficiary of a family heirloom or one of our cherished mementos. When we donate to charity shops, our prized possessions may take on new life as treasured finds for someone else and ease the job of clearing out that will fall to others if we should have the misfortune to be hit by a bus tomorrow.

Especially with no children to nudge us, we will also need to decide on our living arrangements. How long can we negotiate the stairs? Do we want to have the decision to leave forced upon us, or will we make practical new arrangements now, before we find ourselves in trouble?

As we and our peers age, such issues become a natural topic of conversation, but talking is one thing, moving quite another. Many of us will want to stay in our own homes as long as we can manage and keep as much of our lives intact as we can. Our financial situation, our health, and our wealth in relationships cultivated over the years will determine how we live in the final season of winter.

38

Key Quality: Self-Fulfilling

At the end of each day, we can look back and reflect on what has gone well, what could have been better, and how fulfilled we feel by the work we have done, the contacts we have had with other people, the company we kept with ourselves.

Towards the end of our lives, we will want to feel content with how we have approached the good and bad times, the joys and inevitable hardships. Many parents derive satisfaction not only from their own actions but to some extent from the roles their children and grandchildren fulfil in the world. Those of us who don't have that source of contentment need to develop a larger capacity for finding fulfilment in what we bring to the table ourselves.

We came to Earth with a purpose, or at least that is what I assume. Others, like Simone de Beauvoir and her existentialist friends, are convinced that there is no purpose to life other than the one we give it.

Whatever our take on this fundamental issue, those of us who have remained childless or have chosen to be childfree need to feel satisfied with what we have done and who we have become and are still becoming. Our lives need to be self-fulfilling.

The fulfilment can be anything, from the satisfaction of continuing to work and be productive, the joy of going fishing or the contentment of helping out a neighbour to reading a book or following a sports event. Being or becoming self-fulfilling is an essential ingredient for the quality of the years we have left. No one will fulfil our lives for us; no one ever could, not even our partner—if we have one, good friends, siblings who care, or youngsters, whether they are family or not. In this season, we build the last supplies for our old age, and one of them is our capacity to enjoy ourselves on our own, to be fulfilled with how we fill our lives.

Winter

Contemplation and Completion

That time of year in which the birds migrate to warmer regions and all turns quiet as nature withdraws into herself. No growth, this season, but a pause, a lull, a turning within. The time of life when we reflect on who we have been and practise the art of releasing, whether we want to or not. With memories to treasure, our lives quiet down—we quiet down. Until all is quiet as we withdraw.

39

A Life Worth Living

The American software consultant I interviewed told me about an exercise he did ages ago that has stayed with him his whole life. The participants in the workshop he was in were asked to write their own eulogy, then deliver it to the class, speaking about how they wanted to be remembered. He was in his forties at the time, unmarried, with no children. He cannot recall exactly what he said about himself. "Something about being a person people can rely on, a problem solver, a friend. A good guy."

What he does remember vividly is the difference between the eulogies given by those participants who had children and those who didn't.

"As someone who had chosen to remain free from ties that bind, I was struck by everyone who was a father or mother having the primary focus of their eulogy be about their family, and especially being there for their children. The folks who had children didn't mention much of their professional life, their personal growth, or their spiritual path. It was all about how their kids would view them, and how they wished first and foremost to be thought of as a good mom or dad."

The experience still fascinates him, even now that he has, as he says, "inherited a whole tribe of parents, children, and grandchildren" through his primary relationship of over 15 years.

He was struck by the fact that people with families predominantly see themselves through the eyes of that relationship, deriving much of their value from how their offspring is doing, whilst those who do not have families and children have a very different way of seeing themselves, focusing more on their own growth and accomplishments, rather than on the people in their lives.

In 2009, Australian Bronnie Ware wrote a short blog post on what she had learned from people she cared for in their homes in the last weeks or months of their lives. As a result of bare-bones honest conversations at their bedsides, she had begun to see patterns of what people looked back on with misgivings and listed a top five of regrets of the dying.

The first regret, she wrote, was that people deplored having conformed to the expectations of others and not having been true to themselves. Many, she found, hadn't realized half of their dreams. Now, with death on their doorstep, they became clear on how they had short-changed themselves all along.

The second most common regret she noted was one voiced mostly by men. They had come to realize that they had too often prioritized work over being with their wife and children.

Number three on her list was the heartache of people who hadn't expressed their feelings because they had been afraid to upset the apple cart. They wished they had spoken up and clarified issues, instead of pretending these didn't exist and leaving them to rumble like underground volcanoes.

Fourth, people wished they had stayed in touch with old friends. They regretted not having taken the time to get in touch around important life events and letting these friendships slip.

Finally, according to Bronnie Ware, people in her care felt sorry that they hadn't let themselves be happier. She observed that only towards the end of their lives did many realize that being happy is an actual choice and they had allowed themselves to be hemmed in by social conventions and fear of change. They had been content but, ultimately, they would have liked to have laughed more, to have been lighthearted and let their hair down.

Her concise list went viral. Encouraged by this response, Bronnie Ware expanded her blog into a best-selling memoir, *The Top Five Regrets of the Dying.*

"I was convinced that if I lost three pregnancies, my destiny in this life was not to have children, and I accepted it without regrets or pain or disappointment. I thought of adopting a homeless child, but the response from my family and friends was not supportive and I then helped that child to be adopted. Now that I am over sixty, I have no regrets for not having children, and I am happy because I have been able to use my time exploring and learning from other cultures. In this journey, I was able to help children by creating a school for them in a country where going to school was very difficult."

—Woman, 67, health and healing, Canada

Going down Bronnie Ware's list, it would seem that those who have not gone the parenting way might have an easier time once we come to the end of our days. Many of us who chose to be childfree will have braved expectations of family and friends by not procreating and staying true to what was on our inner film reel. If children weren't given, we will have made a conscious choice about what was important to us, what would give us a sense of purpose and meaning, and gone for it. We might have spent our life working, but not at the detriment of spending time with our children, so no regrets there.

I cannot speak to the point of having had the courage to address painful issues, but living an unconventional life anyway, I wouldn't put it beyond us to have had the courage to speak up. If we didn't, there might still be time. Also, many of us will have had ample time for friends and people, old and young, whom we met on the way and liked.

Finally, have we let ourselves be happy enough? In my survey, however unrepresentative, people without children proved to be "bizarrely happy", as the researcher put it, regardless of their age. They weren't waiting for the end of their days to experience joy and gratitude.

40

Leaving a Legacy

Philosophers have thought about death as long as we humans have been contemplating our transient existence. Religions each have a story of how the world originated, as well as an explanation of the mystery of how we transform when we die. Spirituality has its own answers, and many of us live with the idea that nothing remains once we have taken our last breath.

In his 2008 book *Staring at the Sun*, Dr Irvin Yalom, then in his late seventies, admits to being as terrified of death as the next person. Following the teachings of Epicurus who lived around 300 BC, the esteemed former professor of psychiatry is convinced that the dark shadow of death lies at the heart of many of our anxieties.

Drawing on the wisdom of this ancient Greek philosopher and others, Dr Yalom proposes to his patients that they confront the notion of their inevitable passing head on instead of ignoring it. In their sessions with him, he invites them to face the harsh fact that at some point our bodies and memories falter, our lives shrink, and our past will perish with us.

In his decades as an existential psychiatrist dealing with death anxiety, and as a man who will die in the not-too-distant future himself, Yalom has found the concept of "rippling" singularly powerful. Rippling, as he describes it, is the way in which each of us, often without being conscious or cognizant of doing so, creates concentric circles of influence that affect others.

When we give it a moment's thought, most of us will easily remember people who have affected us. Sometimes these are authority figures, like a teacher who kindled our curiosity, an aunt who was understanding, or a boss who recognized our potential. When we grow up, we may meet peers who say just the right thing at the right time.

In turn, we have thrown our own stones into the pond, causing ripples that reached others. We may learn from an old classmate or college friend how our attitude at the time inspired them. We may glean from someone we mentored in their first days on the job how what we told them has guided them throughout their career. We may never hear from people again, but if we do away with modesty for a minute, we can surely list a number of people whose lives we have touched with what we said or how we acted.

> "Thinking of how I stand in the world of families, I believe you don't have to have had your own children to make a positive influence in someone's life and to feel that we have an impact on society or the world. To contribute, to leave a legacy...."
>
> —Woman, 65, artist, Canada

As we approach the final stage of our lives, the question of what we leave behind becomes more acute. We all know it isn't about how much money we made, but rather about what we were able to do for others.

With her 2014 book *The Female Assumption: A Mother's Story*, Melanie Holmes wanted to make her contribution to freeing women from the view that motherhood is a mandate. A mother of three herself, she goes to bat against the outlook that every person must procreate or all they do in their lifetime is for naught. She has even heard the latter uttered about Oprah Winfrey, who, she reminds us, has helped establish 60 schools in 13 countries, has supported women's shelters, built youth centres and homes, and has inspired thousands, if not millions around the globe to take life into our own hands.

She cites the example of the Irish novelist Maeve Binchy, who was known for her descriptive characters and her interest in human nature. Also a playwright, short story writer, and columnist, Maeve

Binchy has sold more than 40 million copies of her novels in 37 languages. Yet when she passed away, in 2012 at age 72, her obituary in *The Daily Telegraph* read, "Binchy would have been a better writer had she been a mother, giving her a deeper understanding of human nature."

Melanie Holmes goes to town against this narrow-mindedness and advocates a broader view of the legacies we leave. Lovingly, she paints the picture of her brother, who died at age 50. He never had any children of his own, but to her mind he did not live any less a full life, just because he opted out of the title of Dad.

The greatest legacy we leave is that of our presence, our authenticity, and the rippling effect we have had on the people we meet, the initiatives we were involved in, and the work we did. If we have been able to be with people in their joys and their despair, if we have opened metaphorical doors for others in our personal life or our professional capacities, if we have been a *mensch*, as the Yiddish expression goes, this is our legacy.

41

Our Will

A song I would love to have played at my funeral is "If It Be Your Will" by the singing poet Leonard Cohen, who died in 2016:

> *"If it be your will*
> *That I sing no more*
> *That my voice be still*
> *As it was before …*

Before thy will be done, however, we need to make a will of our own. Without children as natural inheritors and executors of our estate, who are we designating both to inherit and also clear out all our possessions?

In her 2015 book *Gifted by Grief*, Jane Duncan Rogers describes how her worst nightmare came true, when her husband Philip was diagnosed with stomach cancer. He had three children from a previous marriage and had had a vasectomy before the two of them met that could not be reversed.

Still convinced that women should have children, she had bemoaned never becoming a member of "the mother club". Jane had looked into IVF and found that too invasive physically. She had looked into adoption and found that too invasive emotionally. She didn't have older childless women to talk to, and for a long time, she thought of herself as being weird. Her overriding concern throughout was that she wouldn't have children to look after her when she died.

One day, when she was bewailing her fate, she heard a voice as clear as anyone's saying, "It was never going to be your job this time around. Leading a spiritual life is your job now."

She turned around to find no one there and decided to discover more about this voice. The pair of them moved to Findhorn Foundation in Scotland, where they became an active part of the spiritual community. Then he was diagnosed with cancer, and she had to face what she has always feared: she was going to be on her own, a woeful childless widow.

One day, while Philip struggled with his illness and his sense of letting everyone down, an American friend, a specialist nurse, emailed them a list of practical questions.

"Does Philip want to be buried or cremated?"

"Does Jane know his passwords and user names?"

"Who would Philip like around him when he dies?"

Philip was reluctant at first to get down to such nitty-gritty, but aware of what a huge difference this practical information would make to her later, Jane pushed on.

Taking yet another step in admitting that he was truly dying, they began at the beginning with "What kind of coffin would you like?" (to which, he replied that any old box would do).

It got tough when they came to who he wanted to leave his personal items to. They stuck to the list, and the hours they spent on it proved to be their final project.

"Feeling a great sense of achievement afterwards," she writes. "We were very close, connected, and loving. It ended up being a couple of hours of slightly macabre enjoyment."

> "I am helping a friend raise two grandchildren, ages 5 and 9. They have been in my life for four years. I love them deeply. They do fill a hole I have in my heart."
>
> —Woman, 68, nurse practitioner, United States

In her practical guide *Before I Go*, Jane Duncan Rogers has expanded the list into 140 questions that, when answered, constitute a comprehensive end-of-life plan. The list is on my desk printed and ready for filling in. Yet, somehow, it has landed at the bottom of my pile of papers without commanding my immediate attention. I may get away with saying that I am not yet in the winter of my life and that I am in good health, but who am I trying to fool? Filling out the questions may not be a total pleasure, but it may also turn into an exercise of such honesty about who and what we value in our lives that it provides pointers for what we still want to do and who we want to see more of.

I broach the question of making a will in my interviews. Friends who take great pride in their home and all the books and art they have collected tell me they have picked a charity as their primary beneficiary. She has no siblings, and thus no nieces or nephews who could be executors; he does, but he doesn't want to bother them with this task. So these two will leave it to the public notary to empty their house, sell their possessions, and make sure as much as possible goes to the charity of their choice.

Sara Zeff Geber, PhD, wrote a book on retirement planning for solo agers. As an example of a simple and intentional legacy long before being ready for the embalmer, in a recent article for *Forbes*, she described the thoughtful action of a woman named Tess.

A storyteller early in her career, she had assembled a lovely collection of children's books from the 1950s and 1960s. Having no one in her family to leave them to, she decided to bequeath them to the Ronald McDonald House, where she had sporadically volunteered. She even had a sticker made, "This book was a gift from Tess Miller." Books, tools, and jewellery may all find their way to people within or outside of our family, before our will is read.

An American friend, who was married once for about three weeks, as she says, happens to be in the woes and throes of rewriting her will. She, too, doesn't want to lay the burden of settling her affairs on the shoulders of her siblings or their children, none of them living close by.

That is why, nearing 70 and still travelling the globe for her business, she is in the process of clearing out her home and settling her affairs so that a third party can find what they need in case of emergency. She could name her business partner of almost four decades as the executioner of her estate, she deliberates, but that wouldn't be congruent with their roles in the company, since she has always been the more practical one. She might resort to engaging a professional fiduciary, but she isn't quite ready yet to make that decision. Then there is the healthcare proxy to think about.

Other matters to consider are whether we wish to be cremated or buried, and if so, where? Is there a family grave an executor needs to know about? Do we want to leave instructions for our funeral, including a list of people we would like to be notified of our passing? Will there be a funeral?

A Dutch childfree woman well into her seventies has long ago decided that she will make her bodily remains available for scientific purposes. Her mother did so, as well as her partner, who died five years ago. The medical profession is grateful to receive corpses for students to practise on, or for research purposes.

Whilst the medical profession may cheer, this may mean that there will be no casket and no funeral.

"Who would speak?" says this determined lady, who has already lost a good many of her dearest friends. "If my remaining friends want to say something, they can organize a get-together and serve good food and wine. I have made a provision in my will for that."

The rest of her estate will be divided between her one nephew who lives abroad and a number of friends who can use something extra.

If it be your will . . . For many of us it takes willpower to address somewhat eerie questions we'd rather postpone. We are still healthy, we tell ourselves; we don't need to occupy ourselves with these matters. Yet we may also know people who have been landed with a labour of love because someone close to them didn't think ahead before they died.

"We are but creatures of a day," to cite the title of another of Irvin Yalom's thought-provoking books of tales on psychotherapy. This one he dedicated to Marilyn, his wife of 60 years.

The poetic expression "creatures of a day" he borrows from Marcus Aurelius, the Roman emperor of the 2nd century AD, the last of the so-called five good emperors. The whole quotation is:

> "All of us are creatures of a day;
> The rememberer and the remembered alike.
> All is ephemeral."

42

Polar Opposites

ris Apfel was born in 1921 in New York. She never expected people to know her name or recognize her face. With her short-cropped white hair and big black glasses, she never expected to become a cover girl or the face of a cosmetics company at age 90 or to create her own line of clothing at age 94 and have a documentary made about her life.

She never expected anything, she writes in her book *Accidental Icon: Musings of a Geriatric Starlet,* published in 2018 and which she dedicated to her darling Carl, with whom she shared 68 years of her colourful existence.

Yet there is nothing accidental about the way this nonagenarian has gone about her life. She professes that she just does what sounds interesting and exciting and worries about it later. In the same breath, however, she states that doing new things is tiring. It takes energy and strength. It's easier to just go with the flow, but that is not very interesting, so she works at keeping an open mind and a sense of humour.

This "geriatric starlet", as she mockingly calls herself these days, has worked hard all of her life. Attracting attention with her outgoing personality and outrageous clothes, this dynamo set up her own interior-decorating business. In 1951, together with Carl, she went into replicating as closely as possible antique fabrics in handmade designs. The flamboyant couple would spark interest by wearing clothes made from their sample fabrics. Amongst their most esteemed clients was the U.S. Commission of Fine Arts, which employed them to do restoration work in the White House for nine presidential administrations, from Harry S. Truman through to Bill Clinton.

Travelling all over Europe and northern Africa for their business, Iris Apfel bought clothes and accessories from designers and flea markets. Combining the expensive with the cheap, with arms full of bracelets, she created a style of her own. In her mid-eighties, this landed her an exhibition in the Metropolitan Museum of Art in New York of more than 80 of her outfits and hundreds of accessories, still leaving her more than enough to choose from.

All this travelling is part of the reason the couple didn't have children. In her characteristically candid way, Iris Apfel has said that she doesn't believe in a child having a nanny, so that was not what they were going to do. She has also remarked that "having children is like protocol. You're expected to. And I don't like to be pigeon-holed".

> "I had always expected to have children but didn't feel ready until my forties. It's ironic that some of my partners in my twenties and thirties very much wanted children, but it didn't feel right at the time. In my forties, I was ready for and wanted children and a committed life partnership. I found the right partner, and she didn't want children. It took us three years to work through that issue. I fully released the desire for children with some sadness and a sense of relief and embraced a life without children (as far as I know). I don't have any regrets."
>
> —Man, 70, foundation director/consultant/investor, United States

Her book is full of advice that I hope to remember when I get to be her age. "If you want to stay young, you have to get up in the morning, move beyond the pain, and think young" is one. "Although I'm in my nineties, I still feel like five and a half, because I always look at the world like I'm discovering it for the first time" is another.

She has found that work is healthy for her. Since her beloved Carl died, she works even more to take her mind off his absence, and sometimes she pushes herself too hard. She finds that it is true that getting old isn't for sissies. Her credo is, we start falling apart but we just have to buck up and paste ourselves together. We have only one trip, she writes, and the present is all we have got. The past will not come back, and the future hasn't arrived yet, so her advice is to live each day as though it were our last. And one day we will be right.

The self-appointed geriatric starlet loves her racks and racks of clothes and cupboards full of necklaces, bracelets, and rings. She adores the abundance of cushions, stuffed animals, beautifully upholstered furniture, and artefacts in her home. She still gets a high from dressing up, cruising a flea market, and slipping into a freshly made bed with crisp, clean sheets.

Iris Apfel's lifestyle couldn't be more different from that of a man on the other side of the globe: the 14th Dalai Lama, who was born in 1935 and owns nothing. The considerable income he generates through his books and his speaking engagements is all given to charitable foundations. In his view, the purpose of life is to find happiness, and the ultimate source of happiness lies not in money, power, or status but within us.

As the Dalai Lama describes in *The Book of Joy,* a collection of dialogues between him and Archbishop Desmond Tutu of South Africa, he gets up at 3 a.m. each day. As soon as he wakes up, he remembers Buddha's teaching: the importance of kindness and compassion, wishing something good for others, or at least to reduce their suffering. Then he remembers that everything is interrelated, which is the teaching of interdependence. He sets his intention for the day: that this day should be meaningful. To him meaningful means to help and serve others, if possible, and if that is not possible at least not to harm others. That is what constitutes a meaningful day.

The Dalai Lama and Archbishop Tutu have been good friends for years, but that doesn't mean they agree on everything. While the Dalai Lama thinks we can learn to have control over our emotions, Archbishop Tutu sees emotions as arising spontaneously without us having much control over them.

The latter highlights how the way we face what seems to be negative in our lives determines the kind of person we become. For instance, if we regard the hardships of old age as frustrating, we will become squeezed and tight and angry. His teaching is that, in the midst of the pain, we can recognize the gentleness of the one who is looking after us. But he concedes that sometimes the pain can be so intense we do not have the capacity to do that. The Dalai Lama advocates compassion towards others, so that we forget our own pain. Although the two spiritual leaders come from different angles, they agree on the need to move away from being self-centred towards having compassion in our dealings with others.

The Dalai Lama offers a further nuance. "We have to take care of ourselves," he says, "without selfishly taking care of ourselves. Foolish selfishness means you think only of yourself, don't care about others, bully others. In fact, taking care of others, helping others, ultimately is the way to discover your own joy and to have a happy life. So that is what I call wise selfishness."

The archbishop has the last word. "You are wise. I wouldn't just say wise selfish. You are wise."

> "None of my close friends have children; all for very different reasons. None of them, to my knowledge, have any regrets. The only concern that I, and some of my friends, have is fear of old age if I should lose my partner as well as my mental faculties. I have financial security but no one that I consider the perfect executor of my will or whom I would trust implicitly to care for me should I become incapacitated. But I am working on that."
>
> — Woman, 72, retired dentist, United States

We will all negotiate the final season of our lives in different ways, depending on what we need to stomach, what we believe, and who we are. Archbishop Desmond Tutu has four children; Iris Apfel and the Dalai Lama have none, but they have support systems around them. The Dalai Lama will be well taken care of, once he can no longer fulfil his duties. Iris Apfel no doubt will have as many caregivers as she has bracelets on her arms.

Not all of us are in such a fortunate position as these paragons of our time; still, we can copy their attitude. Both the geriatric starlet in New York and the venerable Dalai Lama in his residence in exile in India are what are known as "positive reframers". Their bones hurt, their knees give out, their eyes are sensitive, but they don't complain.

They remain curious. They use whatever adversity comes their way as a stepping stone to bounce back from, with humour and a sense of wonder. As diametrically different as they appear to be, these two elders also define success in a similar way: giving back to others is what life is about, and both of them continue to do so.

43

Elder Orphans

Fortunately, the issue of how we will live into our old age is not a private one alone. Scientists, civil servants, and politicians are signalling that with the increasing numbers of people who practise childless living, care needs to be arranged in new ways.

In the United States, for example, the mission of the AARP is to empower people to make choices in how they age. The organization was founded in 1958 by then 72-year-old Dr Ethel Percy Andrus, who never married and had no children.

Reputedly, Dr Andrus's one piece of advice to people who dreaded retirement was, "Don't." This retired high school principal, the first woman to occupy that role in California, took her own advice. Alarmed by the lack of financial security of her former colleagues, and after finding many doors closed in her face, she was able to forge a deal with an insurance company to take on retired teachers. After she tirelessly developed additional programs, other trades approached her, and the non-profit became open to all Americans.

The founding principles are still the same: to promote independence, dignity, and purpose and enhance the quality of life for older persons and to encourage older people to serve and not to be served. This organization is part of the IFA (the International Federation on Aging) and has for decades been engaged in advocacy at the United Nations, where it plays a leading role in working with government representatives, businesses, and NGOs to champion the issues of global ageing.

One of their recent studies concerns the growing gap between the number of seniors who will need care and the available supply of caregivers in all countries with low reproduction rates.

According to this study, in 2010, every person over 80 had seven potential caregivers. The expectation is that this figure will drop to four in 2030, and to three by 2050. With the rate of solo agers expected to rise from today's almost 20 percent of the baby boomer generation, the study also points out things that work in our favour. Since we didn't shoulder the considerable costs of childrearing, theoretically we have had decades to save more of our income for our later years. We have also theoretically had more time and space to form strong, long-lasting bonds with friends and build up a network of close, non-familial relationships as well as with nieces and nephews or other younger relatives.

This is the theory. In practice, many of us, with our unconventional streak, may not have felt compelled to enter the rat race in order to provide for a growing household and thus will not have made and saved the money. We may have cultivated close family and non-familial relationships, but not all of us are social animals.

> "I never wanted children . . . well, maybe once for a few minutes when I saw a child put his arms around his mother's neck. From an early age on, I saw myself in a profession, perhaps teacher or journalist. In the 13-year relationship I had with my ex, we never discussed having children. I had a Reiki session shortly after we'd split in which I had visions of mourning children I'd lost in past lives. That made sense to me—that in this life I never desired them."
>
> —Woman, 65, social work administrator, United States

In her article "Childfree Seniors: Taking the Future into Your Own Hands", Laura Dixon, editor at Caring.com, notes another benefit of childless living. As we hit retirement age, we have more freedom to choose where we'll live, as we have no children and grandchildren to bind us to any one place. Nonetheless, most of us—figures from the United States estimate 90 percent; a European survey undertaken in Spain comes to over 80 percent—intend to stay in our own homes as long as we can. If that isn't possible, we would like to remain in the same neighbourhood, where we expect to have networks of friends and acquaintances. In addition to organizations and governments at all levels making studies and recommendations, senior citizens like us are also taking matters into our own hands.

One example is the Village to Village Network. This innovative grassroots non-profit, run by volunteers, started in Boston some 20 years ago. A group of friends realized they might need support if they wanted to stay engaged in their own neighbourhood. Looking beyond conventional solutions, they agreed to help each other as they got on in years, and soon 200 such Villages had sprung up across the country.

Professor A. Sharlach of UC Berkeley, who analyzed the model, saw the potential for reduced social isolation and increased wellbeing and confidence in the ability to age at home. He also warned that such intentional villages were no panacea for vulnerable members of the senior community or people with serious health issues. Still, another 200 such Villages are in development, and an app is available now to facilitate matching requests and volunteers.

Another option that is gaining popularity is cohousing. In such an arrangement, a group of seniors or multi-generational residents live in an intentional community made up of homes clustered around shared public spaces specifically designed to meet both the changing needs of youngsters or families as well as seniors. Old and young, and all in between, participate in activities, meals, and events. In an ideal situation, seniors help youth with their homework, teach them "the old ways", and walk the dog at their own pace, when the children are at school and the parents at work.

An 88-year-old Dutch woman I visited at her home in The Hague is part of a similar community. Of her four siblings, one had had two children and another adopted two children; the other two remained childless like her. With her husband deceased for 36 years, she has been a widow longer than she has been married. Tears well up in her eyes when this decorated volunteer on boards in the field of affordable housing remembers how he always encouraged her every step of the way, and she feels his support to this day.

After his passing, she decided she had better find an environment in which she could grow old with people around her, so she joined the group that together purchased 18 of the 55 flats in a residential building. They have a common room for weekly Thursday coffee and organize outings together, but she hasn't yet brought herself to ask anyone to accompany her to the doctor's office. She still drives her car and appreciates having her independence as long as it lasts. "You will manage," her husband had told her on his sick bed, giving her a confidence that she is still grateful for.

With our growing numbers, we also become an attractive target group for new services to assist seniors, many of them online. These include helping us downsize by sorting through our possessions, moving house, and getting settled in a new place; driving us to friends' houses, a museum, or the doctor's office or hospital; finding volunteers to help with jobs around the house or provide company for an afternoon; or serving as live-in caregivers.

Artificial intelligence (AI) is also addressing the issue, and new robots may come into our lives, such as the robotic dog AIBO, which was first launched in a beagle-like rendition in 1999. The 3,000 models made for Japan and 2,000 for the United States sold out 20 minutes after the web shop opened. Notwithstanding sales of ever-improved models in wider varieties of shapes and colours, Sony discontinued the production of the programmed pet in 2006. In 2018, however, the company launched a new model, complete with a wagging tail, a happy bark, and an endearing face to greet us upon awakening.

AI is also well on its way to introducing androids who can act as butlers, serving us tea and coffee, offering companionship, and conversing on topics of interest. Robotic vacuums, such as Roomba, which clean the home automatically, are already selling well and are popular with young and old.

Studies of human-robot interactions show that a large proportion of participants have a favourable opinion of robot companions as assistants or servants, but only a few want them as actual companions. This may be due to unfamiliarity. When such robots are able to learn and adjust their behaviour based on our unique personal likes and dislikes, we may come to like them better.

Dr Raja Chatila of the CompanionAble project, whose participants include 18 participating groups from seven European countries, notes that robots can learn from subtle cues. We lean forward to pick up the newspaper from the floor, and next time they will do it for us. In the near future, a mobile robot with an avatar-like face will bring us our medication at the exact minute we need to take it and analyze data on the state of our health. Robots will learn that we take turns in conversations, so they can interact with us in a natural and intuitive way. The aim of this EU project is to create likeable companions to help the elderly remain independent in an intelligent and automated household, or smart home, with similar advanced research projects run in other parts of the world.

Carol Makak, a contributor to SeniorCare, the American online senior information clearing house, describes herself as "an ageing advocate". In her 2016 series of articles in the Huffington Post, she discussed how she is planning for her own elderly years.

She confesses to not having planned well, although she realizes that adults like herself, who live without a spouse or children, cannot afford to put it off. Her parents delayed to make arrangements, she writes, but they had four children they could rely on for care. She doesn't, and nor do her sister or many of her friends. She uses the descriptive terms "elder orphan" and "adult orphan" for people without relatives to care for them. She attributes this term to Maria Torroella Carney, MD, an internist, geriatrician, palliative care physician, and public health leader, who is doing research on our growing demographic, in order to get experts talking about new support programs for single or widowed seniors without children.

Carol Makak has good advice for all of us who wish to remain independent for as long as we can: Apart from eating healthily, staying fit, and keeping our brains sharp, she astutely suggests we make friends with supportive types.

44

My Winter

I may change my tune once it is my turn to surrender to the discomforts of old age and imminent death, but I have long surprised friends by saying that I look forward to the moment of passing. Of course, my body will be terrified, as it will perish, but the essence of me, I believe, will live on and be reunited with the One.

The metaphor I use is the sea; however, I will tell you upfront that whilst it helps me as a theoretical model, it doesn't quite fit.

When the waves crash onto the shore, drops spring up and fall back into the wholeness of the water. I see our lives as such a drop. We loosen ourselves from the whole for a moment in time, our physical life span here on Earth, then we fall back into being part of the whole again. A drop of seawater as such is never to be found again, and this is where my analogy doesn't work, as I believe that the energy of our particular essence remains distinguishable, at least for some time after our passing.

> "Women (and men) need to know that they have options to having children, that it's not something they must do for their family or society. Many people give less thought and planning to having children than to buying a car."
>
> —Woman, 72, proof-reader and retired librarian, United States

I was raised the modern way, without a faith of any kind. Even on his deathbed, when he began to feel the presence of his mother, my father firmly believed that he came from nowhere and wouldn't go any-where after death.

We had a wondrous conversation, he and I, on the day he survived the euthanasia injection administered in accordance with the strict guidelines here in the Netherlands. His GP had discussed his medical prognosis with him: an aggressive brain tumour that had been partly removed but was growing back fast and impairing him in lots of ways. Radiation was no option, since it would have minimal effect on the tumour but would leave him lethargic and drained of all energy. An impartial second doctor had come to verify that my father had con-sidered the matter deeply and made a conscious choice to die a few weeks before death would come to fetch him.

My family was all for this procedure and had been astounded when I said I was not. If my father wanted this and my mother consented, I would not object, of course, and my siblings asked me why I wasn't in favour of this modern-day method of alleviating suffering at the end of life.

I explained my belief that we are consciousness come alive in a human body, so I expect that there is a lot to be gained in terms of awareness when we can die consciously instead of being sedated or euthanized. Since my father was not in pain, he had the chance of going over in a conscious state, so I did not want to take that away from him.

My parents held no such belief, and an afternoon was picked.

Gathered around my father's bed, we said how much we felt he had loved us, how much we had learnt from him, how grateful we were that he had been our father. He joked that there were no hidden bank accounts for us to discover after his passing. One after the other we kissed him goodbye. The good family doctor went in with his black case, and we waited in silence, until he came back with pursed lips—not his favourite part of the job.

We went in to sit with my father, who was still breathing. We sat, and we sat some more, as his breathing didn't cease. Then he opened his eyes and asked for a glass of beer. He felt a bit drowsy, he said. When the doctor came back to establish his death some time later, that is how he found him—sitting up in bed, propped up by cushions, with a glass of beer he had barely nipped from. We decided that we couldn't go through this procedure again, so we would wait for the inevitable end.

Later that warm summer evening, when I sat by my father, he asked, "Did you give me a good funeral?" When I said we hadn't had his funeral yet, since he had not died, he shrugged. I said that I was alive, and with me talking with him, he must still be alive, too, but that did nothing to convince him. His eyes went to the paintings on the wall. "I must admit that it is curious that the same paintings that hang on my living room wall are now with me in death," he said pensively, and fell asleep.

He died in peace, and we gave him a good funeral. I still feel his presence and envision him sitting on the chair across from me. I see him in his sixties, full of vitality, curiosity, and zest for life. His body was a one-time event, but in my perception his spirit is eternal.

I like my father's presence here with me at my writing table, in front of the window where pigeons, neighbouring cats, and blackbirds come to visit in the garden. My deathbed, if I have one, will be very different from his, with the four of us coming as often as we could. The last years of my life will be different from my mother's with, again, the four of us coming as often as we can. Some of the people I spoke to worry about this last phase, an equal number of others don't. We will cross that bridge when we get to it.

> "I would have been happy if I had had children. I am happy now that I didn't."
>
> —Man, 71, entrepreneur, the Netherlands

As our bodies become less agile, and the scope of what we can manage shrinks, we have to gradually practise the art of letting go. We are all like the ancient Sumerian goddess Inanna, goddess of warfare and love, whose myth of going into the underworld and coming back from death has been told and embellished since long before we began counting the years.

Although she is the goddess of sexuality and power, she is not considered the patron of marriage, nor is she viewed as a mother. Young and impetuous, Inanna is constantly striving for more power than she has been allotted. Having taken over the domains of several other deities, she wishes to conquer the underworld where her older sister Ereshkigal resides as queen.

Under the pretext of wanting to attend the funeral rites of her sister's deceased husband, Inanna dresses ornately, in a turban, lapis lazuli necklaces, fine garments, a pectoral, and a golden ring. When she pounds on the gates to be let in, Ereshkigal instructs the gatekeeper to close the seven consecutive entrances. He is to open them one by one at a crack to let her sister enter, but only after she has shed a royal adornment at each gate.

At the first, she is asked to hand over her lapis lazuli measuring rod, and so it goes, until she appears before her sister naked. Inanna performs the feat of coming back from the dead as some of us do, too, when we are given up by modern medicine and yet, somehow, return to life.

The story of Inanna shows us that we cannot bring anything with us on our last journey. We leave this earth plane as naked as when we came. The goddess shedding the ornaments of her worldly identity exemplifies how we all have to concede the symbols of what constituted our life and our identity.

The first to go is our measuring stick, as our opinion still counts and we may still vote but it's younger people now who run the schools, the restaurants, the businesses, the country, the whole she-bang. We know we are past our prime, once DJs start to announce music that we danced and kissed to as "golden oldies". We wonder in our old age if doctors have finished their studies, as they seem so young, and that new president, too, looks like a rookie. Stories about the time we were young may still find an eager ear if we tell them well, but we definitely make ourselves unpopular when we interject, "Well, in our time . . ." too often, when youngsters tell us about exploits that, for the life of us, we can't see the use of.

"I felt there were enough children in the world already. Better spend my life supporting those."

—Woman, 70, translator and teacher, the Netherlands

My best bet of negotiating this last phase of life with elegance and dignity is to live by the one law, two engines, and four principles of Open Space.

Open Space Technology came into being as the result of a joke made out of frustration, according to originator Harrison Owen in his 1997 book *Expanding Our Now*. Having organized an international symposium with esteemed speakers, he kept hearing from people that they had had the most interesting conversations during the coffee breaks. He decided to run his next project as one big coffee break: no programme, no speakers, just rooms and times and questions that people wanted to talk about.

The experiment worked. People organized themselves into groups around topics close to their hearts. Harrison Owen had found what he had been looking for: a better way for humans to engage with each other about their concerns. Over time, he formulated the one law and four principles that guide the process, which have helped me stay relaxed in challenging situations since I learned about this method.

His "two engines" are Passion and Responsibility.

People have objected to the first term, "passion", wondering if it couldn't be called "interests" or "concerns". I myself would like it changed to "curiosity", as that is what gets me out of bed in the morning, but Harrison Owen has stuck with Passion.

The second engine that drives an engaged process is Responsibility, as this will ensure that passionate concerns will be converted into action. Without responsibility, passion can be whimsical; with it, openings can be created for innovation and things can get done. Translated to our senior years, no one else can be responsible for the quality of our lives. We will have to make sure we remain passionate or curious and take responsibility for how we engage.

The one law of Open Space is what is known as the Law of Two Feet, which says, "Whenever you find yourself neither contributing nor learning, use your two feet."

Anyone who has ever been to a party knows how this one works. People float from one group to another until they find the company they click with. No offence intended if we move on, none taken. This is the secret of everyone having a good time—whether we dance like mad or sit in a corner conducting a serious conversation. The Law of Two Feet reminds us that life wants to flow and not stay stagnant behind a façade of conditioned politeness. This is not in any way a plea to be rude. It is a reminder to take responsibility and place ourselves where we have most to contribute or most to learn.

On now to the principles.

The first is "Whoever comes are the right people." This one has helped me greatly when I have organized evenings and conferences. Although there were budgets to meet and marketing to be done, this maxim took away needless worrying and replaced it with faith, which is a much nicer feeling to work from. I expect this to help me, too, when the time comes that I am housebound due to poor health. If I have no visitors for a while, I intend to think that whoever comes are the right people, so if no one comes, that must be right, too.

The second is "Whatever happens is the only thing that could have." Now this is a spiritual teaching if there ever was one. No use crying over spilt milk or water under the bridge. A full yes to contemplating lessons learnt, but a strict no to complaining about how things ought to have been or how they could be different. Everything in our lives, the good and the bad, the ecstatic and the horrendous, is the only thing that could have happened. We have to deal with it on an inner level, but we can only do so when we accept what was and what is. I find great beauty in this second principle, even in the face of all that is unjust and hurtful in this world of ours. It is as it is, and with our curiosity and responsibility we are to take it from there.

The third principle is "Whenever it starts is the right time", which recognizes that we don't have to wait for an official to signal when to begin. We can start conversations about what matters to us anytime, at the bus stop or the cash register, provided we don't take too long for the busy people in line behind us to start shuffling their feet and hissing over our senescent shoulder. Our life, too, began at exactly the right time.

The fourth principle is its complement, "When it's over, it's over." For group gatherings, this means that once the energy has gone out of a conversation, people don't need to stay together out of politeness or habit. In our own lives, this is a memento mori like no other.

Whether we believe we will go on to an afterlife or it all ends with our final breath, when it's over, it's over—meaning no lamentation that we die too young or live to be too old. It is what it is, a harsh and beautiful truth. Our life began when it began, whoever we met were the right people, whatever happened was the only thing that could have happened, and when it's over, it's over.

45

Getting Ready to Go

Kind people gave me names of octogenarian and nonagenarian family members who never had children. Some have email addresses, so I could ask them questions online; others I called or visited.

One day I drove out to see an old friend of my mother's who has lived in Belgium for the past three decades. She and her husband were the only ones in my parents' circle of friends in the suburb where I grew up who had no children. Weekdays turned the quiet village into a mother-and-children's zone, as men disappeared for the day and life revolved around us children. I gather this must not have been easy on her at the time.

We sit with tea and cake, and she tells me about her days. Her mornings start with reading the Bible and contemplating a daily text she receives via email. "I take great interest in those observations and reflect on them during the day," she says.

I admire her for even being on email, but she shrugs her shoulders. "I am also on social media, but I don't post anything. I just look at the pictures of young people I know to keep up to date with their adventures."

Thin and frail, she is dressed immaculately in off-white slacks, a crisp shirt, and a cardigan draped over her shoulders. She pours more tea and says, "You have to stay active, even if you have to force yourself. Last year, when I fell and broke my hip, I could have let go of walking, but I chose not to be felled. I went to physiotherapy, I performed my exercises, and now I am able to move about quite well again."

I ask what gives her pleasure in the long days when she doesn't see anyone but her caregiver. She tells me that she enjoys the changes in nature that she sees from her window—flowers unfolding, trees changing colour. She reads the newspaper on her iPad and prays for people who live in dire circumstances through wars or natural disasters. "My faith is a source of support and joy for me," she says, "and every day I pray it might be so for others, whatever their religious beliefs."

She loves playing Wordfeud online with nephews and nieces and with someone new she met through that game. She marvels that this is possible these days. Also, she is on the telephone a lot—with her favourite niece, who never had children, either; with children of friends who sought her out when they were younger and with whom she has stayed in touch. "I say 'children,'" she laughs, "but like you, most are now in their sixties."

We go back to the conversation about her faith. "The closer I come to death, the more I feel God is there for me," she says.

She considers herself fortunate that she has been able to outlive her husband, who had slowly lost his faith. The last months of his life were actually quite beautiful, she tells me. Only very seldom had they touched on their childlessness. That had been a lonely path, but they hadn't wanted to hurt each other more than necessary. In his dying days, her husband said how he had admired her for never complaining and always seeing the positive. She was touched and told him she could return the compliment. "Now that I am alone, it serves me well to have learnt to feel a sense of loneliness and not be done in by it."

This 91-year-old, who has since passed, has been a friend of my mother for over half a century. In all those years of friendship, the two of them have never touched on the topic of whether she had wanted children or not. My mother has wordlessly assumed that her friend suffered a great invisible loss and had felt compassion for her having missed what constituted the fulfilment of her own life.

"I always wanted children, but slowly it dawned on me I couldn't do it. I subbed high school for dozens of years, and I've loved and helped a multitude of kids and don't feel like I've missed anything."

—Woman, 70, high school teacher, United States

On a winter's day, I visit the childless aunt of one of my childless friends at her flat in an assisted living facility that offers cleaning, meals, and nursing assistance, if needed. It's easy to see where this 92-year-old former nun usually sits, as one big chair has a reading lamp overhead and a low table of books next to it. Within easy reach are Krishnamurti's *You Are in the World* in its Dutch translation and *La Doctrine Supreme* and *In Touch* by John Prendergast.

"Have you read that one?" she asks, and when I shake my head, she highly recommends this book on authenticity and the natural sense of truth in our body.

She shuffles a bit since taking a fall six months ago, but she has been to the bakery to get us her favourite chocolate biscuits. After she has made tea, she extinguishes the light in that part of her one-bedroom flat, and thus we sit, me in her reading chair with the lamp, as darkness falls.

She has cat's eyes, she says, so she can see well in the dark, which served her well during her time in the convent, with its long, silent, sparsely lit corridors. She likes sitting in the dark. As evening falls, she enters a contemplative state in order to experience the great mystery, that all that seems so different is an emanation of consciousness. Moving beyond the ego and its stories, she travels deeper, to the solitude of the eternal all, the unity that gives rise to all that is.

I ask her if she realized that she would not have children when she became a nun, but this was not at all on her mind at the time, she says. At age 21, unsure of where to find the depth of reflection she was looking for, she was awoken early one morning by a voice that asked, "Do you want to experience solitude with me?" She had never thought of entering religious life before but at that moment felt this was her way.

After two years of deliberation and visits to several monastic orders, she opted for a Benedictine abbey that offered daily hours of solitary study as well as a practice of Gregorian chanting. At age 23, she disappeared behind bars for a life dedicated to Spirit.

She loved it at first, but through the years she came to another understanding of the godhead as not one of the divine above and us below but as one eternal, all-encompassing lifegiving Spirit. She had taken holy vows, so it took her some years to come to the point of stepping out. She never regretted her time as a nun, she says, nor her decision to go back into the world, where she was now free to deepen her practice of unity consciousness.

After 17 years behind closed doors, at the age of 40, she moved to Amsterdam, where she landed in the revolutionary Sixties. She met a former monk, took the pill, and got married. They would have liked to have seen the product of their love, she says, but the two of them deemed themselves too old.

Alongside their jobs, the pair immersed themselves in Tibetan Buddhism and self-development. A widow for the past 12 years, she looks back at her life with great satisfaction, concluding that every step was as it should be, and she looks forward to death as a release into oneness. In the meantime, she sits and reads and contemplates the beauty of the trees in the garden below, the ever-changing shapes of things, and the impermanence of what we call I.

Evening has fallen when our conversation draws to a close. This is how I leave her—a being of light sitting in the dark, contemplating our finite existence on this earth plane and enjoying every moment of it.

I can only hope that, if I reach her age, my nieces and nephews will still come to visit and offer support, and that I will have as rich an inner life as these wonderful elderly women, who, during their life spanning almost a century, have seen cultural views regarding the childless broaden to include all kinds of life experiences. I certainly hope in the years still given to me on this planet that people who are childfree by choice or childless by circumstance anywhere in the world can feel proud of our self-directed lifestyle and can rejoice in our rich, self-fulfilling lives.

A List of Books

I am happy to share with you the books that I found most inspiring, insightful, and entertaining whilst researching and writing this one. I have listed them in order of the year in which they were most recently published and given brief descriptions of their content.

Accidental Icon: Musings of a Geriatric Starlet by Iris Apfel
  (HarperDesign, 2018)
  She never wanted to be an old fuddy-duddy, so even now when she has to overcome the pains of her aged body, exuberant style icon Iris Apfel maintains her joie de vivre. In this visual memoir, she relates how she became a black-belt shopper, how she and her beloved husband of 68 years, Carl, ran their famous fabrics business, and how her old age is saved by her curiosity and sense of humour. "You have to be interested to be interesting" is a credo she has lived by for almost a century now.

Before I Go: The Essential Guide to Creating a Good End of Life Plan by Jane Duncan Rogers (Findhorn Press, 2018)
  If you had died yesterday, what would you have wanted to happen, who would you have liked to be there, and how would you have liked your possessions to be distributed? Most of us avoid answering these questions, but if we have no children, we make it much easier on siblings, nieces or nephews, friends or officials to deal with our estate if we have left instructions. The trick is not only to read this book but to take the

time to actually sit down, write down our wishes, and give a copy to the people we'd like to perform a function after we've gone.

The Mother of All Questions: Further Reports from the Feminist Revolutions by Rebecca Solnit (Haymarket Books, 2017)
This feminist book addresses rapid social changes, such as our understanding of consent, power, rights, gender, representation, and voice. In the opening essay, American writer, historian, and activist Rebecca Solnit unpacks a notion that she is confronted with wherever she goes to give talks, i.e., that there is only one proper way for a woman to live. A champion weaver of storylines, she fulminates against the presumed one-size-fits-all formula for a good life, whilst love comes in so many forms and can be directed at so many things.

Baby Debate: Everything You Need to Consider Before Becoming a Parent by Diane Polnow (CreateSpace Independent Publishing Platform, 2017)
As an adoptee, this author's mission is to help others make sure they are willing and able to create the ideal circumstances for a child to be born into. As a psychologist, she has done extensive research in what it takes physically, emotionally, and financially to raise a child. Neither for nor against people having children, she paints a realistic picture of one of the biggest commitments we can make in our lives. Worth the read, if you're considering having a child. The author has also developed pre-parenting guidebooks and workbooks, available on her site www.babydebate.com.

Other than Mother: Choosing Childlessness with Life in Mind by Kamalamani/Emma Palmer (Earth Books, 2016)
Until recently Emma Palmer called herself Kamalamani, the name she was given at her ordination as a Buddhist in 2005. Slowly it dawned on this British counsellor, body psychotherapist, and author that childbearing is not compulsory but a choice. Discovering that she first and foremost wants to serve all of life and not necessarily one or more children of her own, she has come to a place of equanimity. With honesty and sensitivity, she traces her own journey with this highly private decision against the backdrop of overpopulation, environmental degradation, loss of biodiversity, and a society that is still mostly pro-natal.

The Book of Joy: Lasting Happiness in a Changing World by His
Holiness, the Dalai Lama and Archbishop Desmond Tutu with
Douglas Abrams (Hutchinson, 2016)
In April 2015, Archbishop Tutu travelled to meet the Dalai Lama at his
residence in India for a week of conversations. These have been collected
and published in this book and offered as a gift for others. The dialogue
between these two spiritual giants of our time centres on the purpose of
life, avoiding suffering, and discovering joy that doesn't depend on circumstances. It's a gem to take in hand and read cover to cover or in bits
and pieces.

*Selfish, Shallow, and Self-Absorbed: Sixteen Writers on the
Decision Not to Have Kids,* edited and with an introduction by
Meghan Daum (Picador, 2015)
Between them, the 16 contributors to this anthology cover most of what
there is to think, say, and feel about not having children. Where one
writer actively wanted not to have children, another wished for them
when her partner didn't and was no longer able to have one when her
next partner did. Author and sometime columnist Meghan Daum has
made a clever compilation that challenges the notion that non-parents
are what the title says.

Creatures of a Day: And Other Tales of Psychotherapy by Dr Irvin
D. Yalom (Piatkus, 2015)
Dr Yalom is a parent of four, but in this book about ageing and facing the
end of life the prolific emeritus professor of Psychiatry at Stanford University and practising psychiatrist tells the tale of quite a few patients
who have remained childless. In his signature sensitive yet humorous
style he portrays ten people who, each in their own way, are coming to
terms with death—their own and that of beloved others.

Spinster: Making a Life of One's Own by Kate Bolick (Corsair, 2015)
This New York Times best-seller is both a personal memoir and a cultural
essay on how women move through the world alone. Having harboured
a "spinster wish" since youth, Kate Bolick wondered if she could spend
her life alone and still be happy. In this original book, she philosophizes
about how conventional life is still organized around marriage and
parenthood, and about the joys of being alone. For her muses and role

models, she depicts the lives of poet Edna St. Vincent Millay, essayist Maeve Brennan, columnist Neith Boyce, novelist Edith Wharton, and social visionary Charlotte Perkins Gilman, whom she calls "my awakeners".

My Life on the Road by Gloria Steinem (Random House, 2015)
Writer, activist, organizer, co-founder of Ms. magazine, Gloria Steinem is an advocate of listening as a skill to practise. She gets her information from fellow airplane passengers and taxi drivers, local organizers, and women—many women. The story is always different up close, and even now, well into her 80s, she still travels. In this memoir, she shares memories of her itinerant youth, which taught her that adults weren't necessarily tied to one spot. Being on the road also stands for the freedom she has always allowed herself and that she, as a radical feminist, would want all women to have in determining their own lives.

Gifted by Grief: A True Story of Cancer, Loss, and Rebirth by Jane Duncan Rogers (Wild Wisdom, 2015)
As her husband lay dying of cancer, the author had to face up to her worst fear coming true: she was going to be a childless widow past child-bearing years living on her own. With excerpts from her own and her husband's diaries, the Irish author, who lives in the Findhorn Foundation Community in Scotland, tells the story of coming to terms with remaining childless, losing her husband, and having a first-hand experience of the golden light he walked into. The appendix contains a checklist of practicalities to address before dying. See also www.beforeigosolutions.org and the author's TEDx Talk.

The Birth of the Pill: How Four Crusaders Reinvented Sex and Launched a Revolution by Jonathan Eig (MacMillan, 2014)
This witty, well-researched tale of four pioneers who brought us "the pill" reads like a novel. Fiery Margaret Sanger was a legendary crusader for birth control. In 1950, at age 71, she sought out the eccentric Dr Gregory Pincus who was (in)famous for his experiments with in vitro fertilization. Her request to him was simple: develop a pill. He recruited gynaecologist Dr John Rock, a staunch Catholic promotor of voluntary parenthood, who researched the effects of hormones on fertility. Katharina McCormick, one of the world's richest women and an ardent

supporter of Planned Parenthood, funded the project. The pill first became available in 1960.

The Female Assumption: A Mother's Story: Freeing Women from the View that Motherhood is a Mandate by Melanie Holmes (CreateSpace Independent Publishing Platform, 2014)
"Motherhood is a path that, once embarked upon, must be followed through to completion," writes Melanie Holmes. Dedicating the well-researched book to her daughter, this mother of three set out to describe the bumpy road of motherhood so that women can evaluate whether having children is for them. Writing from an American angle, the author wishes to help free women from the view that motherhood is a mandate, and that every person must procreate or all they do in their lifetime is for naught.

What I Know for Sure by Oprah Winfrey (MacMillan, 2014)
This gilt-edged hardcover is a compilation of 16 years of columns by the woman who turned making conscious choices about our lives into prime-time television. In the same penetrating manner she is wont to use with her guests, she talks about her own struggles with overwork and over-weight, her warm friendships with people who give her advice, and her deepening into the awareness of mortality and the essence of being.

No Kidding: Women Writers on Bypassing Parenthood edited by Henriette Mantel (Seal Press, 2013)
This anthology contains 37 open, honest, poignant, and short observations by women writers on why they are childless or childfree. They didn't dare love someone so much, they didn't know they would be good parents, their profession always came first, they remained ambivalent and the choice was taken for them, or they never wanted to parent in the first place. As Beth Lapides, host and creator of UnCabaret, writes, "Not having kids is saying a big no—no to the same thing over and over and over, so that you can say yes to everything else."

Living the Life Unexpected: 12 Weeks to Your Plan B for a Meaning-ful Future without Children by Jody Day (Bluebird, 2013)
Using a mixture of autobiography, case studies, social history, and self-help, this English author blends the personal with the practical to sup-port childless-not-by-choice women to move forward. Her own experience of discovering that she couldn't have a child because of "unex-plained infertility" she found hard, lonely, and scary. She has now built an online platform, Gateway Women: United by and Beyond Childless-ness, where women can share their stories and learn from each other how to find out who they are when they drop "the baby story." See also her 2017 TEDx Talk.

The Faraway Nearby by Rebecca Solnit (Granta, 2013)
When Che Guevara didn't put a glove on to shake a woman leper's hand, that beautiful woman with the little-understood disease felt seen as a per-son, and the encounter blew both of their hearts open and changed the course of their lives. How we meet, how we enter and influence each other's life stories and ultimately, how we can be there for each other in times of need is the topic of this tour de force of a book. It all starts with a mound of apricots from Solnit's mother's garden who, as a result of dementia, needs to be moved to a care home; the discovery of cancerous cells in her own breast that need treatment; and seeking a fragile balance, as the author tries to preserve as many of the apricots as she can.

Confessions of a Childfree Woman: A Life Spent Swimming against the Mainstream by Marcia Drut-Davis (self-published, 2013)
The author was overjoyed when she found out that her husband didn't want children. However, telling her in-laws on national television in the mid-seventies proved traumatic. After a life of "swimming against the mainstream", as she puts it in her subtitle, this now 75-year-old woman tells the story of how she has been true to herself in a time when not hav-ing children was stranger than it is now. The appendix has a list of sup-port organizations and resources for childfree people in the United States. She also organizes childfree groups to go on cruises together.

The Top Five Regrets of the Dying: A Life Transformed by the Dearly Departed by Bronnie Ware (Hay House, 2012)
Australian Bronnie Ware is a free spirit who for several years worked as a palliative caregiver. As a good listener she started to see patterns in what the people who came to the end of their lives told her. When the post she wrote about the top five regrets of the dying went viral, she decided to expand it into a book. She is an author now and a musician, a mother, and most of all someone who leads by example of how it is to follow our heart and be authentic.

The Baby Matrix: Why Freeing Our Minds from Outmoded Thinking about Parenthood & Reproduction Will Create a Better World by Laura Carroll (LiveTrue Books, 2012)
Laura Carroll is an active voice on the childfree choice. With a Masters in Psychology and Communications, she has tracked and researched the topic over the last 15 years. In this book, she challenges pronatalism, i.e., the idea that parenthood and raising children should be the central focus of every person's adult life. She addresses this powerful set of beliefs, which dates back many generations by debunking assumptions of normalcy, destiny, fulfilment, and elderhood. The subtitle for this feisty book is apt.

Savvy Auntie: The Ultimate Guide for Cool Aunts, Great-Aunts, Godmothers, and All Women Who Love Kids by Melanie Notkin (William Morrow, 2011)
This dynamic author, speaker, and lifestyle expert realized that she didn't know the first thing about becoming an aunt when this great gift came her way. Learning that nearly 50 percent of adult women in the United States are non-mums, she wrote this guide. From sizes for cute clothes to tips on how to help a child grow emotionally, this is a go-to book for taking delight in the role of the extra adult in a child's life whilst remaining free to lead your own life. See also SavvyAuntie.com as well as the author's website for ongoing research on the power of what she coined as PANK® (professional aunties no kids). Inspired by her life in New York, her 2014 book with the clever title *Otherhood* is a funny and vulnerable memoir on how today's career women find a new kind of happiness in life.

Committed: A Skeptic Makes Peace with Marriage by Elizabeth
Gilbert (Riverhead Books, 2010)
After the journey of finding herself that she described in her best-selling
Eat, Pray, Love, this author knew one thing for sure: she had found the
love of her life, but she never wanted to marry again. The United States
Department of Homeland Security, however, had their own ideas about
her Brazilian-born Australian man's comings and goings. He is allowed
to come and stay only if they get married. Delving into marriage as an
ever-changing institution, and examining her own resistance to it as well
as her wish to remain childless, the author turns another episode of her
life into a finely carved description of our time.

The Forgotten Kin: Aunts and Uncles by Robert M. Milardo
(Cambridge University Press, 2010)
Remembering the importance of his uncles as role models, this social
scientist started to interview uncles and nephews about their relationship, whilst on a visiting research sabbatical in New Zealand. Back at the
University of Maine, he expanded his research to include aunts and
nieces. This first academic and engaging study of what Dr. Robert
Milardo calls "aunting and uncling" shows the long reach of these affec-
tive intergenerational relationships. The web of the family is woven
tighter as aunts and uncles, nephews and nieces mentor each other and
cultivate their friendship.

Two is Enough: A Couple's Guide to Living Childless by Choice by
Laura S. Scott (Seal Press, 2009)
"Why did you get married if you didn't want kids?" This seemingly innocent question got Laura Scott researching the growing minority of the
North American population who could have had children but made a
decision not to. She gives facts, quotes scientists, and tells the stories of
the people she interviewed, as well as her own. This is a good companion
for those who feel lonely and sometimes clueless about why they would
be perceived as a threat as they don't do what most do.

Silent Sorority: A (Barren) Woman Gets Busy, Angry, Lost, and Found by Pamela Mahoney Tsigdinos (BookSurge Publishing, 2009)

She believed in hard work, perseverance, and playing by the rules, so she felt like a failure when she didn't conceive and needed to reinvent herself in the long shadow of infertility. This American author describes her own journey through the five stages of grief—denial, anger, bargaining, depression, and acceptance—as identified 50 years ago by Elisabeth Kübler-Ross. On her website, she offers constructive advice for involuntarily childless women and couples who often choose not to speak about their plight.

Stepmonster: A New Look at Why Real Stepmothers Think, Feel, and Act the Way We Do by Wednesday Martin, PhD (Houghton Mifflin, 2009)

Stepchildren can and do affect a remarriage, sometimes for the worse. Wednesday Martin, who holds a degree in Comparative Literature, married a man with two daughters. Drawing on anthropology, sociology, evolutionary biology, and feminist literary and cultural theory, she wrote this informative and validating book about the complex dynamics in complicated families. Through this book, I found the beautiful article on Andrew Solomon's website entitled "On Having a Mother Who Loves Opera" (2006), in which he describes in detail his often contradictory feelings about becoming a stepson to a woman who couldn't be a better partner for his father.

No Kids: 40 Good Reasons Not to Have Children by Corinne Maier (Emblem Editions, 2009)

After 13 years of "maternal humiliations", French psychoanalyst and mother of two Corinne Maier wrote a quick and candid book about the delusions of motherhood. Listing 40 reasons not to have kids, such as "Kids are the death of desire" and "Motherhood is a trap for women", Maier's booklet created immediate controversy and a media storm.

Staring at the Sun: Overcoming the Terror of Death by Dr Irvin
   D. Yalom (Jossey Bass, 2008)
The distinguished emeritus professor of Psychiatry at Stanford, author
of definitive textbooks on his trade and novels, is as afraid of death as
anybody. Using the ancient philosopher Epicurus as a guide, he believes
that the frightening thought of inevitable death is at the heart of much
of our anxiety. Illustrated with conversations with his patients, he shares
his experience of coming to terms with mortality and oblivion.

*Misconceptions: Truth, Lies, and the Unexpected on the Journey to
   Motherhood* by Naomi Wolf (Vintage, 2002)
Newly married feminist Naomi Wolf longed for a baby and became pregnant whilst taking contraceptives that had never failed her before. Honest
and open, she traces her journey through the American health system as
well as her inner joys and blues. Talking to friends she discovers how little
they all know of what is ahead, medically and emotionally, and how little
the culture allows mothers to speak about their doubts, agonies, and
resentments.

*Families of Two: Interviews with Happily Married Couples Without
   Children by Choice* by Laura Carroll, with photographs by
   Krista Bartz (Xlibris, 2000)
Knowing she did not want children, Laura Carroll wanted to learn about
the roadmaps of long-time, happily married couples who had chosen not
to parent. She interviewed 100 heterosexual couples across the United
States, conducted in-depth interviews with 40, and conducted in-person
interviews with 15 selected for publication. As different as the couples
were, she found they had all considered their decision carefully; many
did not model traditional gender roles, and all found a life without
children to be fulfilling. A good read for those wanting to know how
others "do" their childfree marriage.

Expanding our Now: The Story of Open Space Technology by
   Harrison Owen (Berrett-Koehler Publishers, 1998)
This is a book about a novel, utterly engaging way of having meetings,
gatherings, and conferences. The reason it has made it onto this list is
because I have adopted the practice of the "two engines, four principles,

and one law" that guides this self-organizing process in my own life. For instance, the second principle, "Whatever happens is the only thing that could have", is a spiritual guideline to accept what is, whatever it is. The dual engines of Passion and Responsibility help avoid this turning into a form of fatalistic thinking. Quite the contrary—this is a recipe for an engaged and engaging life.

Japan: The Childless Society? The Crisis of Motherhood by Muriel Jolivet (Routledge, 1997)
While working as a professor of French and Sociology at the Sophia University in Tokyo, Muriel Jolivet interviewed Japanese women about their experiences of marriage and motherhood. Women confined to home and childcare knew little about the old ways, she discovered, and assumed that their baby needed to be perfect. They worried themselves sick and started to resent their child, their working husband, and their life. Younger generations tended to find marriage unappealing and even shunned relations with the opposite sex, leaving politicians to worry about the declining birth rate in this ageing society.

Beyond Motherhood: Choosing a Life without Children by Jeanne-Safer, PhD (Gallery Books, 1996)
In the 1990s, it was more unconventional than now to make the conscious choice not to have children. Psychoanalyst Jean Safer believes in rigorous self-examination. After applying her skills to her own situation and reaching the conclusion that motherhood was not for her, she sought out women all over the United States to talk about how they made this decision and how they shaped their lives. Two decades on, this is still a sweet read for those currently engaged in the process of deciding whether or not to have a baby.

The Loss That Is Forever: The Lifelong Impact of the Early Death of a Mother or Father by Maxine Harris, PhD (Penguin, 1996)
Some events are so big and so powerful they cannot help but change everyone they touch. When a child loses a parent, that child grows up feeling different and alone. The death of a young mother or father, whether it was sudden or came at the end of a long illness, divides

childhood into a clear "before and after". All subsequent development, all later happinesses and disappointments begin with the reality of death and loss, a reality that remains, no matter how much time passes. Recommended reading for those who find themselves in such a situation.

Pronatalism: The Myth of Mom & Apple Pie edited by Ellen Peck and Judith Senderowitz (Thomas Crowell, 1974)
Parenthood is neither a universally desirable and inevitable condition nor a prerequisite to a full life but a vocation for which only some of us are suited by aptitude or choice. That is one of the innovative suggestions offered in this compilation of 24 articles written by scientists, journalists, and role models. Their aim is to introduce the word "pronatalism" into the general vocabulary to describe the "hidden persuaders" which encourage reproduction and exalt the role of parenthood. They refute the notion that woman's destiny is closely wedded to the birth experience and flag the danger that choice is not really free in a prejudiced cultural context.

The Female Eunuch by Germaine Greer (1971; paperback relaunch by Harper Perennial Modern Classics in 2006)
The proper subject for love is one's equal, this outspoken Australian feminist wrote in this plea for freedom for women to be a person with dignity, integrity, passion, and pride. The central tenet of the book is that men hate women, though the latter do not realize this and thus are taught to hate themselves. Mixing irreverence, humour, polemic, and scholarly research the book catapulted this academic onto the scene, and she has never left.

The Feminine Mystique by Betty Friedan (1963; paperback edition by Penguin Classics in 2010)
In the 1950s, a "real woman" found complete fulfilment in caring for her husband, their children, and the house—at least according to the myth. When she found that life unfulfilling, Betty Friedan carried out her own research amongst the well-educated women she went to college with and found pervasive malaise and frustration behind the front door, sparking the "second wave" of the women's feminist movement in the United States. Think Betty Draper. The writers of Mad Men must have used this book for their research.

The Second Sex by Simone de Beauvoir, new translation by
Constance Borde and Sheila Malovany-Chevallier (original
French edition 1949; new English translation published by
Jonathan Cape in 2010)
Finally, the seminal work of this French philosopher was translated into
English in a way that does it justice. In 1953, an abridged version had come
out, but the translation lacked all of the poetic flow in which De Beauvoir
expands on the myths and laws and the economic and social systems that
have elevated man and downgraded woman over the ages. After all these
years, it is still a joy to read this learned and rich 800-page volume with
which De Beauvoir hoped to contribute to humanity, letting go of the
eternal strife between the sexes in order to reveal its authentic meaning
and discover the true form for the human couple.

A Big Thank You

In the beginning, there was my mother. Having found happiness as the wife of one and mother of four, she had assumed that her eldest daughter would follow in her footsteps.

I, however, questioned her life from the get-go. Growing up in the 1950s and 1960s, to my youthful eyes my father's comings and goings looked far more attractive than her housebound existence. I never decided *not* to have children, but following my lifepath took me further and further away from family life.

I thank my mother for forcing me to articulate my choices, as she would regularly question me as to why, in heaven's name, I wouldn't marry and start a family. Now 90 years of age, she remains convinced that I would have found ultimate fulfilment in a life like hers, although she grudgingly concedes that I seem incomprehensibly happy.

I am profoundly grateful to my brothers and sister and my in-laws for having procreated. My nieces and nephews are very close to my heart. I very much enjoy our dialogues on whether or not to have children, especially now that the years in which it "should" happen are upon a number of them.

Thank you, especially, Stephanie Schuitemaker, for being so engaged with my research and writing, and for introducing me to 30-somethings willing to explore this tender topic.

Thank you, Nina Schuitemaker, for your feminist views, which always broaden my perspective.

My gratitude also goes to good friends who supported me through-out the process of writing this particular book.

Inviting me to one of her Proprioceptive Writing workshops when I got stuck, Wies Enthoven helped me find my voice with this topic. Marilyn Hamilton, Marinet Ritz, and Marise Voskens supported me with their keen interest in the angles I was taking. Thank you, Anneloes Timmerije and Charles den Tex, for conversations about the art of writing, the benefits of a dull life for a writer, and the necessity of having to let go of wanting to be liked when a book requires solitude. Thank you, Caroline de Gruyter and Carolyn Lee, for sending me articles from the many newspapers and magazines you read. Thank you, Jim Garrison and Wim van Droffelaar, for your boundless confidence in me and what I have to say.

I am indebted to the authors who have already written about this tender topic. Thank you for the information and inspiration, for your honest self-examination and fiery advocacy. I especially wish to express my gratitude to Laura Carroll and Marcia Drut-Davis for the articles you alerted me to through your tweets.

At Findhorn Press, I am grateful to Sabine Weeke for wanting to take this subject on and thinking with me about potential ways to approach it. Thank you also for that one long conversation, when I thought I wouldn't be able to get all my material organized in a coherent and engaging way. Much appreciation, too, to Inner Traditions, the new mother company of Findhorn Press, for your immediate enthusiasm about bringing the grand option of child-less living to a wider audience. Thank you, Nicky Leach, for our precise ping pong game to get to the final version, with i's dotted and t's crossed and all of my Dutch English corrected. Thank you, Nicki Champion and Geoff Green, for your hand in the design of the cover and layout.

How lucky I was to run into data researcher Marian Dragt, when I was wondering how best to advance my idea of a worldwide survey. I could only stare in admiration when you organized all of the questions I had compiled into categories and in what seemed like no time, created a professional survey easily accessible on all kinds of devices. Thank you for bringing your expertise to the topic and for presenting the data to me in a way I could work with. I could not have done this book without you.

Fortune smiled upon me, too, when Aimée Warmerdam again consented to put her excellent editing skills at my disposal. Picking up on a remark about how childless living changes with the seasons of our lives, she encouraged me to try and organize the content according to that timeline. This stroke of genius made all of what I had written before fall gracefully into place. I am also grateful for your thoughtful feedback on aspects that I missed or could enhance or clarify, and on darlings to kill, of course.

Deep thanks to the good people from 30 countries who gave of your time to take the survey and add your comments—some of you I know; most of you I don't, as you are friends of friends, or you found the link through social media. *Grazie mille* to Nicoletta Nesler and Marilisa Piga of the Lunàdigas project, for getting so many of your fellow Italians to participate in the survey. Thank you, Manish Jain, for connecting me with women in India, and you, Elaine Harrison, for introducing me to The Silver Tent on Facebook. Thank you, too, members of the international networks of women entrepreneurs, United Succes and Business Women of Egypt 21, for your confidence, chats, and referrals.

I'm grateful for all the conversations I have had on this intimate topic. Many exchanges were somewhat in passing. At dinners and parties, gallery openings and events, people took me aside and talked to me when they heard of my current topic of research. I was astounded time and again how little it took for you to confide in me about the why and how of your childless or childfree lives.

In particular, my heartfelt gratitude goes to those of you on the five continents who consented to be interviewed at greater length. You opened up to me—in tête-à-têtes in your home or mine and over Skype—about your choice to remain childfree, your struggles with remaining childless, or your discovery that childless living was indeed your destiny. Some of you hadn't spoken about this topic for years, if ever. For others, it was run of the mill to address this private aspect of our lives. Each of you shed light on the issue in your own way and I think back to our conversations with great fondness.

Thank you, too, parents who spoke candidly to me about the discovery that having children can be hard and difficult and far from the dreamlife it is still portrayed to be.

I pay homage to all those who have thought and written about the intertwined topics of the position of women, feminism, relationships, having children, and the purpose of life. Not being a psychologist or social scientist, I have had my pick of what to use and I have tried my best to do justice to your findings, stories, and opinions. I highly recommend the book selections in my bibliography to readers who wish to delve deeper.

Closer to home, indeed as close as can be, I am deeply grateful to my partner, Jos van Merendonk. After a quarter of a century together, I still marvel at your permanent good humour, your glee that we don't have children or grandchildren and, especially, your artist's understanding of my being with the topic more than with you for months on end.

About the Author

Lisette Schuitemaker is a Dutch author who also writes in English. She has an MA from Leiden University in the Netherlands, where she studied the Classics, and later obtained a BSc in Brennan Healing Science in the United States.

Before becoming an author, she founded and ran a communications agency, which she successfully sold. Until recently, she served as Chair of the Trustees of the Findhorn Foundation in Scotland and of the Center for Human Emergence in the Netherlands.

This is her fourth book on patterns in our lives that underpin our actions but are seldom addressed. Her book *The Eldest Daughter Effect: How Firstborn Women Harness Their Strengths*, was also the subject of her 2016 TEDx Talk.

Lisette loves having no children; living in Amsterdam with her partner, painter Jos van Merendonk, who never wanted children; and keeping in touch with her nieces and nephews and other people, old and young, whom she comes across.

More on Lisette Schuitemaker and her work you'll find at:
www.lisetteschuitemaker.com
Instagram: lisetteschuit & childlessliving
Facebook: lisetteschuit & Eldest Daughter Effect
Twitter: @LisetteSchuit & @childlessl

Further Books by Lisette Schuitemaker

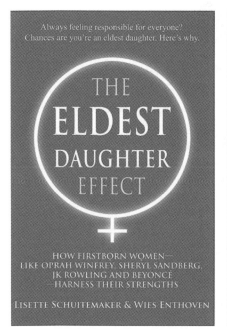

The Eldest Daughter Effect

What does it mean to be an eldest daughter? Firstborns Lisette Schuitemaker and Wies Enthoven set out to discover the big five qualities that characterize all eldest daughters to some degree. And they discuss why, in spite of being more intelligent, verbally proficient, and motivated to perform than their siblings, eldest daughters often doubt they are good enough. This book demonstrates how firstborn girls become who they are, how to give them more freedom, and the best ways to support them.

9781844097074

The Childhood Conclusions Fix

All of us have drawn conclusions in our childhood: impressions about ourselves, the world and our place in it. These childhood conclusions still produce thoughts that mark our behaviors. With examples from her private practice, Schuitemaker shows how childhood conclusions work and how to turn them around into a positive outlook.

9781844097340

FINDHORN PRESS

Life-Changing Books

Learn more about us and our books at

www.findhornpress.com

For information on the Findhorn Foundation:

www.findhorn.org